NANCY HARRIS

Nancy Harris is a playwright and screenwriter from Dublin. Plays include: *Two Ladies*, *The Beacon*, *Our New Girl*, *The Red Shoes* and *No Romance*. Musicals include: *Baddies: The Musical* (book and lyrics with composer Marc Teitler) and *The Magician's Elephant* (adapted from the book by Kate DiCamillo). For television, Nancy is the creator and writer of the BAFTA-nominated comedy-drama series *The Dry*.

Nancy has been awarded The Rooney Prize for Irish Literature, The Stewart Parker Award, and has been a finalist for the Susan Smith Blackburn Prize. She has been both IFTA and BAFTA nominated for her screenwriting, most recently as Best Writer: Comedy for *The Dry*.

Nancy Harris

SOMEWHERE
OUT THERE YOU

NICK HERN BOOKS
London
www.nickhernbooks.co.uk

A Nick Hern Book

Somewhere Out There You first published in Great Britain in 2023 as a paperback original by Nick Hern Books Limited, The Glasshouse, 49a Goldhawk Road, London W12 8QP, in association with the Abbey Theatre, Dublin

Cover image: Photographer: Sarah Doyle; Design: AAD

Designed and typeset by Nick Hern Books, London
Printed in the UK by Mimeo Ltd, Huntingdon, Cambridgeshire PE29 6XX

A CIP catalogue record for this book is available from the British Library

ISBN 978 1 83904 283 6

www.nickhernbooks.co.uk/environmental-policy

An Abbey Theatre production, **Somewhere Out There You** was first performed at the Abbey Theatre, Dublin, on 27 September 2023.

CREATIVES

Cast

Sebastian	Stephen Brennan
Marcus	Oscar Clancy
Brett	Cameron Cuffe
Marcus	Harley Cullen-Walsh
Cynthia	Danielle Galligan
Ensemble	Jess Kavanagh
Casey	Eimear Keating
Pauline	Lise-Ann McLaughlin
Ensemble	Teddy Moore
Gareth/Dave/Ensemble	Donncha O'Dea
Ensemble	Aisling O'Mara
Alan	Enda Oates
Eric	Paul Reid
Tess/Karen	Kate Stanley Brennan

Writer	Nancy Harris
Director	Wayne Jordan
Set Designer	Maree Kearns
Costume Designer	Catherine Fay
Lighting Designer	Sinéad McKenna
Composer, Sound Designer and Musical Director	Sinéad Diskin
Movement Director	Paula O'Reilly
Wigs, Hair and Make-up	Val Sherlock
Casting Director	Sarah Jones
Voice Director	Andrea Ainsworth
Fight Director	Ciaran O'Grady
AV Design	Patricio Cassoni
Assistant Director	Dolores Rice
Assistant Set Designer	Ronan Duffy

COMPANY

Producer	Jen Coppinger
Company Manager	Danny Erskine
Production Manager	Anthony Hanley
Company Stage Manager	Bronagh Doherty
Deputy Stage Manager	Tara Furlong
Assistant Stage Manager	Aidan Doheny
Producing Assistant	Clara Purcell
Head of Costume and Costume Hire	Donna Geraghty
Costume Supervisor	Eimear Farrell
Breakdown Artist	Sandra Gibney
Costume Maintenance	Vicky Miller
Cutter/Maker	Tara Mulvihill
Costume Dresser	Juliana Schmidt Tomazini
Props Supervisor	Adam O'Connell
LX Programmer	Simon Burke
Sound Supervisor	Morgan Dunne
Sound Engineer	Sean McKeown
Radio Tech	Kate Crook
Set Construction	Triangle Productions
	Andrew Clancy
	Gorilla Design
	Crew Metalwork
Scenic Artist	Vinnie Bell
Marketing	Muireann Kane
	Heather Maher
	John Tierney
Press	Stephen Moloney
Social Media	Jack O'Dea
Promotional Image Photograph	Sarah Doyle
Production Photographs	Ros Kavanagh
Irish Sign Language Interpreter	Vanessa O'Connell
Audio Describer	Bríd Ní Ghruagáin
Artistic Director/Co-Director	Caitríona McLaughlin
Executive Director/Co-Director	Mark O'Brien

ABOUT THE ABBEY THEATRE

As Ireland's national theatre, the Abbey Theatre's ambition is to enrich the cultural lives of everyone with a curiosity for and interest in Irish theatre, stories, artists and culture. Courage and imagination are at the heart of our storytelling, while inclusivity, diversity and equality are at the core of our thinking. Led by Co-Directors Caitríona McLaughlin (Artistic Director) and Mark O'Brien (Executive Director), the Abbey Theatre celebrates both the rich canon of Irish dramatic writing and the potential of future generations of Irish theatre artists.

Ireland has a rich history of theatre and playwriting and extraordinary actors, designers and directors. Artists are at the heart of our organisation, with Marina Carr and Conor McPherson as Senior Associate Playwrights and Caroline Byrne as Associate Director.

Our stories teach us what it is to belong, what it is to be excluded and to exclude. Artistically our programme is built on twin impulses, and around two questions: 'who we were, and who are we now?' We interrogate our classical canon with an urgency about what makes it speak to this moment. On our stages we find and champion new voices and new ways of seeing; our purpose – to identify combinations of characters we are yet to meet, having conversations we are yet to hear.

ABBEY THEATRE SUPPORTERS

The Abbey Theatre thanks the following individuals & companies for their generous support.

Gabhann Amharclann na Mainistreach buíochas leis na daoine aonair & na cuideachtaí seo a leanas as a dtacaíocht fhlaithiúil.

PROGRAMME PARTNER

LEARNING & ACCESS PARTNER

BANK OF AMERICA

CORPORATE GUARDIANS

Bloomberg

RETAIL PARTNER

ARNOTTS

GOLD AMBASSADORS

HOSPITALITY PARTNER

THE WESTBURY

IT PARTNER

 Qualcom

RESTAURANT PARTNERS

 HAWKSMOOR

PLATINUM PATRONS
The Cielinski Family
Deirdre and Irial Finan
Sheelagh O'Neill
Susan and Denis Tinsley

DIRECTORS' CIRCLE
Tony Ahearne
Pat and Kate Butler
Janice Flynn
Conor and Elisabeth Kehoe
Elizabeth Papp Kamali in memory
of Lloyd Weinreb R.I.P.
Dr. Frances Ruane

SILVER PATRONS
Frances Britton
Tommy Gibbons
Andrew Mackey
Eugenie Mackey
Eugene Magee
Gerard and Liv McNaughton
The Kathleen Murphy Foundation
Andrew and Delyth Parkes

Thank you to all the above supporters for your continued support of your national theatre. We would also like to thank our generous supporters who have asked to remain anonymous.

BECOME A SUPPORTER OR CORPORATE GUARDIAN OF THE ABBEY THERATRE AND HELP US BRING INSPIRATIONAL WORK TO OUR STAGES, SCHOOLS AND TO COMMUNITIES THROUGHOUT IRELAND.

Our mission is to nurture a love for the art form for the generations to come, mentoring new talent and giving voice to all of Ireland's citizens. If you'd like support us in our work, please contact: **marie.lawlor@abbeytheatre.ie**

For Kwasi

Acknowledgements

My endless love and thanks to Wayne Jordan for his friendship, his artistry, his joy and his unwavering commitment to *Somewhere Out There You* since its inception. It would not be here without him – and possibly nor would I.

My heartfelt thanks and appreciation to Catriona McLaughlin, Jen Coppinger, Mark O'Brien, Jesse Weaver, and all at the Abbey Theatre for their support, encouragement, enthusiasm, and all that they have given to bringing this production wholeheartedly to life.

Many people were instrumental to the development of this play over many years. I would like to thank Anthony Weigh, Erik Ehn, Anne Washburn, Gary Winter, Madeline George, and all who organised and took part in the Stillwright Playwrights' Retreat of 2012 where this play began its life. I would also like to thank Rochelle Stevens, Dave Evans, Cian O'Brien, Project Arts Centre, Nancy Abrahami, Aideen Howard, Louise Stephens, Nick Dunning, the Tyrone Guthrie Centre, Birkbeck University, and all the actors and artists who have taken part in various readings over the years. My love and thanks to Mary-Anna Kearney for a lifetime of friendship and the *Home and Away* theme tune (and Claire and Ruth, who were there too). And lastly I would like to thank my wonderful, ever-loving family: Eoghan, Connie, Mungo, Mir-Kev, Sophie, Kwasi and especially my mother Anne, who believed this play would find a home, even when I'd long given up hope. Thank you.

N.H.

'All stories are love stories.'

Robert McLiam Wilson
Eureka Street

'We don't see things as they are, we see things as we are.'

Anaïs Nin
Seduction of the Minotaur,
referencing Talmudic texts

Characters

GARETH, *headmaster*
MARCUS, *pupil, ten*
KAREN, *Marcus's mother, thirties*
CASEY, *thirties*
BRETT, *Casey's boyfriend, thirties*
CYNTHIA, *Casey's sister, thirties*
PAULINE, *Casey's mother, sixties*
ALAN, *Casey's father, sixties*
ERIC, *Cynthia's husband, thirties*
TESS, *thirties*
SEBASTIAN, *sixties*
DAVE
ACTOR 1
ACTOR 2
ACTOR 3
ACTOR 4

Note on Text

A forward slash (/) indicates an overlap in dialogue.

Parts can be doubled or tripled.

Scenes move quickly and merge fluidly from one to the next.

All stage directions, props and even locations are suggestive, not prescriptive.

This text went to press before the end of rehearsals and so may differ slightly from the play as performed.

Prologue

Darkness.

Then –

A principal's office.

MARCUS, *intricately dressed as Cleopatra, with a large impressive headdress, enters stage-left and quietly takes a seat at the headmaster's table.*

The headmaster, GARETH, *and* MARCUS's *mother,* KAREN, *enter mid-conversation.*

They do not see MARCUS *at first.*

GARETH. Ours is a fragile democracy, Mrs Moriarty, I'm sure you understand that.

KAREN. Yes.

GARETH. Orders, structures, symbols, rules... uniforms. They might be unpleasant, depressing even to some, but they serve a function.

She nods at him, uncertain.

KAREN. Of course.

GARETH. It's all very well to express ourselves and we want the children to be able to express themselves, but if we blow up the things that hold us together, where will we be in the morning, Mrs Moriarty?

KAREN. I don't know.

Beat.

He hasn't been blowing things up, has he?

GARETH. Not literally, Mrs Moriarty, no.

KAREN. Oh thank god.

GARETH. I'm speaking figuratively here of course.

KAREN. Of course.

GARETH. You understand.

KAREN. Yes.

Beat.

Well, no.

GARETH. No?

KAREN. Not – really. What exactly has he done – wrong? Marcus?

GARETH. The attire, Mrs Moriarty.

KAREN. Attire?

GARETH. The outfit. It isn't appropriate. Not for assembly and not for school.

KAREN. Oh.

GARETH. We have to maintain a sense of consistency.

She stares at GARETH, at a loss.

He is going to have to start wearing clothes.

KAREN. What do you mean?

GARETH. Normal clothes.

KAREN.…Is he not wearing – normal clothes?

GARETH *gestures to* MARCUS.

KAREN *follows the gesture and starts.*

Jesus Christ. Marcus!

GARETH. Ah – ha /

KAREN. What do you look like?

GARETH. Well impressively like Cleopatra I would say but it's certainly not the official St Mary's School get-up.

He chortles to himself.

KAREN. But – where did he get these?

GARETH. Which?

KAREN. He didn't leave the house like that this morning.

GARETH. No well /

KAREN. Do you think I dressed him up like that and put him on the bus?

GARETH. Of course not. Although because of the wig and the level of detail –

KAREN. Jesus, Mary and fucking Joseph.

GARETH. Now we don't need swearing, Mrs Moriarty –

KAREN. I think we sure as shit do. Marcus, where's your trousers?

MARCUS doesn't answer.

KAREN begins to circle him pulling at his clothes.

GARETH. Mrs Moriarty /

KAREN. Where's your jumper? /

GARETH. Mrs Moriarty /

KAREN. Where are your Clarks?

She's clearly distressed.

GARETH. Mrs Moriarty, I've been trying to tell you this is not the first time –

KAREN. What?

GARETH. This is the third time this week that Marcus has come to school dressed as Cleopatra?

KAREN. The *third*?

GARETH. Yes.

She looks at MARCUS.

KAREN. You're saying he's been wandering up and down the corridors all week dressed like this?

GARETH. In a manner.

KAREN. Why didn't somebody tell us?

GARETH. I am /

KAREN. Why didn't somebody phone?

GARETH. Well, look I could go into the noughts and crosses of it all and to be frank it's a touch – embarrassing. But in a nutshell, on Monday Marcus's teacher was off sick and the substitute thought he had learning difficulties – which was grossly offensive to the children with learning difficulties, but the substitute was northern so we thought why bother. Tuesday, I'm embarrassed to say they were rehearsing the nativity and god help us the costume department thought Cleopatra was part of it. Don't ask me how they're getting their HDips these days. And today, well today it all came to a rather harsh head.

KAREN. So where's his uniform?

GARETH. Huh?

KAREN. Where's the uniform he left the house in?

GARETH. Well from what I've gleaned from Marcus this morning – his uniform is in a skip.

KAREN. What do you mean it's in a skip?

GARETH. It's in a skip not far from these premises.

KAREN. Marcus Moriarty, I should smack your arse! That uniform cost a small fortune.

GARETH. Mrs Moriarty /

KAREN. I'm absolutely mortified.

GARETH. Well.

KAREN (*to* MARCUS). Why aren't you saying anything?

GARETH. Perhaps an asp got his tongue.

He laughs to himself.

KAREN. An ass?

GARETH. Asp. Like the – that Cleopatra… would you like to tell your mother what an asp is, Marcus?

MARCUS. A snake. Cleopatra kept one on her head.

KAREN. A snake?

GARETH. Indeed. Killed her in the end. She made it bite her. After her beloved Mark Antony died in battle. Or so the folklore goes. She was a profoundly ugly woman, Cleopatra, by all accounts. A far cry from Elizabeth Taylor at any rate, but she had an electric hold over the opposite sex, there seems to be no disputing that.

His gaze lands on MARCUS, *who looks up at him.*

Unfortunate beat.

GARETH *stands up abruptly.*

GARETH. I'm sure Marcus can fill you in on all the gory details about Cleopatra, the real stickler here of course is the why?

KAREN. Why?

GARETH. Why Marcus has suddenly taken to dressing up as Cleopatra and coming in to school. Have a seat, Mrs Moriarty.

KAREN looks at him, suspiciously.

KAREN. Why?

GARETH. So you can sit.

KAREN. I don't want to sit.

GARETH. Please –

KAREN. You're going to blame me.

GARETH. For what /

KAREN. You're going to say it's my fault.

GARETH. No I'm –

KAREN. You are, I know, I can tell by your face.

GARETH. We're not at all interested in assigning blame, Mrs Moriarty. Our first and only concern is the welfare of our pupils and we're just wondering if anything's going on in the domestic – sphere that might have – unhinged Marcus.

KAREN. The domestic sphere?

GARETH. Have you any idea at all why he might be dressing up like this?

KAREN. No.

GARETH. No?

KAREN. No.

GARETH. Well, has he ever dressed up like this before?

KAREN. All kids dress up.

GARETH. Well yes.

KAREN. It's what they do. Marcus isn't any different.

GARETH. That's true, that's certainly – but I think you will agree that Marcus has taken things to the next level here. I mean he seems to have done actual research.

KAREN. Oh god.

KAREN suddenly drops into a seat.

Please don't tell my husband.

GARETH. Pardon?

KAREN. He'll kill him.

GARETH. Kill him!

KAREN. He's said it before.

GARETH. So this has happened before?

KAREN. He's not normally a violent man, don't get me wrong – but one time Marcus tried on my shoes and Colin gave him the most almighty walloping. (*To* MARCUS.) You remember that, don't you, Marcus?

MARCUS *nods.*

Well do you want that to happen again?

MARCUS *shakes his head.*

Then for god's sake stop this nonsense like I told you!

She looks at GARETH, *despairing.*

GARETH. Alright. No. We're – we're not going to have that happen. Marcus, that's not going to happen.

KAREN. He's not a bad man, Colin. He's really not, but there are some things – a little boy in cobalt-blue stilettos, it just pushed his buttons.

GARETH. Right… So how long has he been dressing in women's clothing?

KAREN. Well no, it's not just – women's clothing. It's all clothing really as long as it's – flashy, you know.

GARETH. Flashy.

KAREN. Different. Bright buttons. A vibrant colour. Something vintage. He's always on at me to get him a police uniform. Or a barrister's wig.

GARETH. I see.

KAREN. He just likes –

GARETH.…dressing up?

KAREN. Do you think we should get the doctor?

GARETH. The doctor?

Her voice starts to crack a bit.

KAREN. Is that what you're getting round to?

GARETH.…Actually, I was going to suggest drama.

KAREN. Drama?

GARETH. As a funnel.

KAREN. Funnel?

GARETH. For his creativity.

KAREN *sits back, looks at* GARETH.

But that's something to consider in the fullness of time. As of today we have to look at the sensitivities involved, i.e. your husband, and marry them up with the practicalities at hand, i.e. our rules. And find a way to – navigate. As it were.

KAREN. Which means what?

GARETH. This is going to have to stop.

KAREN. Well of course it's going to have to stop.

GARETH. So without being heavy-handed we'll have to take it in hand.

He seems to soften for a moment, as he looks at MARCUS.

You will have to come to school dressed properly from now on, do you understand that, Marcus?

MARCUS *looks at* GARETH.

You will have to come to school dressed as a little boy.
I mean not 'dressed' as a little boy, you will *be* a little boy.
Come to school dressed as yourself alright, in the regulation uniform and we won't have any further problems. Do you understand?

MARCUS *nods sadly.*

I'm not disputing your imagination, Marcus, I think it's wonderfully engaged.

KAREN. Do you?

GARETH. I think he'll do very well with that sort of commitment.

KAREN. Really?

GARETH. I don't see why not. He's certainly admirably immune to playground taunts – which bodes well.

KAREN. Children can be cruel.

GARETH. So can critics. Who knows to what heights he might one day soar?

He looks at MARCUS, *smiles.*

Then at KAREN.

Well. Very good. We've got a lot sorted out.

GARETH *moves to the door.*

KAREN *stands awkwardly, staring at* MARCUS.

It's clear she is no more enlightened now than at the start.

GARETH *gestures limply to the door as* KAREN *picks an invisible piece of fluff off* MARCUS*'s forehead.*

KAREN. …Do you really think he might have a future ahead of him? You know, in – entertainment?

GARETH. I think he could surprise us all, Mrs Moriarty.

KAREN. That's – good. Isn't it? Is it?

GARETH. I think so, yes.

KAREN. Yes. Okay. Yeah.

GARETH. Well.

GARETH *smiles, wanting them to go.*

KAREN *looks at* MARCUS *again, notices something.*

KAREN. Hey Marcus?… Are those my earrings?

ACT ONE

One

Twenty years later.

CASEY*'s flat. Living room.*

PAULINE, CYNTHIA, ALAN *and* ERIC *perched variously around.*

CASEY *and* BRETT *stand at the centre holding hands.*

An introduction has just been made.

ALAN. Brett?

BRETT. Yes.

CYNTHIA. Not Rhett?

BRETT. No.

PAULINE. Bradley?

CASEY. That's his surname.

ALAN. Rhett Bradley?

BRETT. Brett Bradley

PAULINE. Alliterative.

CASEY. Yes.

PAULINE. Did your parents do that on purpose?

BRETT. Which?

PAULINE. The double B.

ALAN. Oh god.

    BRETT *glances at* CASEY, *smiles.*

BRETT. I don't know.

PAULINE. Cos it's a very strong statement an alliterative name. One doesn't make it lightly.

ALAN. Here we go.

PAULINE. Are you trying to undermine me, Alan?

ALAN. Not at all.

ERIC. He was only teasing.

CYNTHIA (*to* ERIC). Don't get involved.

ERIC. Sorry.

PAULINE. No *I'm* sorry. I think I'm nervous. We've never met any of Casey's boyfriends before. Have we?

ALAN. No.

PAULINE. It's sort of – virgin territory. To coin a phrase.

CASEY. Mom.

PAULINE (*quickly*). Not that she hasn't had any boyfriends. I'm sure she's had hundreds. Thousands, even. Over the years.

CASEY. Mom, please.

PAULINE. We've just never actually – met them.

CASEY. Okay /

PAULINE. She's a very private person you see, Casey. Not like Cynthia.

ERIC. Different strokes for different folks, eh.

PAULINE. That's it, Eric. You always know the thing to say.

CYNTHIA. Does he?

    CYNTHIA *rolls her eyes*.

    PAULINE *leans in to* BRETT.

PAULINE. Eric used to be a television producer.

ERIC. Still am a television producer, Pauline.

PAULINE. Well, yes. Of course you are, pet. Freelance.

ERIC. Free as a bird as I like to put it.

    ERIC *laughs*.

    CYNTHIA *looks away in mild disgust*.

BRETT (*to* ERIC). Oh? What kind of things do you produce?

CYNTHIA. Do we want to be getting into all this?

ERIC. Documentaries mainly.

BRETT. Wow. That's fascinating.

ERIC. Working on a thing about orphans now.

ALAN. Really, Eric? Orphans?

ERIC nods a little proudly.

ERIC. It's about how being orphaned affects a person's life. Their relationships. Their career choices.

ALAN. Hmmn /

PAULINE. And how does it affect them?

ERIC. Not in the way you'd think.

ALAN. No?

ERIC. Cos the conventional wisdom would be that not having parents ruins your life. You know, you've no inheritance, no unconditional love –

PAULINE. Desperate /

ERIC. But actually the orphans I've met seem pretty happy. They've good jobs, nice partners, they don't have to worry about introducing anyone to the mother-in-law –

He winks at BRETT.

They can just 'be'.

ALAN. Right.

ERIC. And most of us don't get unconditionally loved anyway, according to the experts, so the orphans are a pretty happy bunch as it goes.

Beat.

ALAN. And when's this going to air, Eric?

ERIC. Oh well. Not for – I mean it's not definite or anything. I'm still tinkering around with the pitch.

CYNTHIA. Okay we're really not here to talk about Eric's career plans. We're here to meet Brett. Bradley. Casey's new boyfriend. With the alliterative name.

.

CASEY *smiles, pleased they're back talking about her.*

PAULINE. Yes.

CASEY. You gave us both alliterative names.

PAULINE. What?

She points.

CASEY. Me and Cynthia. You gave us both alliterative names.

PAULINE. Oh well, yes of course I did. That's how I know.

ALAN. What?

PAULINE. That it's not a decision a parent makes lightly. Cos a name is an important thing. It creates one's destiny.

BRETT. That's a great way of putting it, Mrs Cassidy.

BRETT *smiles at* CASEY.

PAULINE. We made the right choice with Cynthia anyway, I'm glad about that.

CASEY*'s face drops a bit.*

CASEY. Right.

PAULINE. Oh, love, I didn't mean it that way. It's just Casey's not a romantic name whatever way you look at it.

CASEY. No.

BRETT. It's a very original name though.

ALAN. It is /

BRETT. Not one you hear often.

PAULINE (*to* BRETT). It was my father's surname. We wanted to name her after him.

ALAN. Couldn't very well call her Micko.

PAULINE. So we settled on the latter. Casey Cassidy.

CASEY. I don't think Brett wants to hear about this.

BRETT. I do.

CASEY. It's boring.

BRETT. I want to know everything about Casey.

This stops everyone in their tracks. CASEY *smiles, delighted.*

PAULINE....Really? Well isn't that just – lovely.

CASEY. Would anyone like another drink?

ALAN. Please.

PAULINE. I would've thought you'd had plenty.

ALAN. I've had one, Pauline.

PAULINE. Are you driving?

ALAN. Are you my wife?

PAULINE. Not any more, thank god.

   CASEY *gives him a drink.*

CASEY. Here you go, Dad.

ALAN. Thanks, love.

   An awkward beat.

PAULINE. How's Barbara, Alan?

ALAN. She's fine thank you, Pauline.

PAULINE. Has she had her hip replaced yet?

ALAN. She's not having her hip replaced, Pauline.

PAULINE. Oh that's right. She's thirty-five, I forget.

CASEY. Mom.

PAULINE. What?

   CYNTHIA *moves to change the subject.*

CYNTHIA. Tell us about *you*, Brett.

BRETT. Me?

CYNTHIA. Yes, you. That's why we came here.

   BRETT *smiles, polite.*

BRETT....What do you want to know?

CYNTHIA. Everything. From beginning to end.

BRETT. Gosh. Well.

   CASEY *jumps in fast.*

CASEY. He's a wonderful cook.

CYNTHIA. Really?

CASEY. He made the quiche.

ALAN. You make quiche, do you, Brett?

BRETT. Sometimes.

ALAN. That's – unusual for a man.

CASEY. He can make anything.

BRETT. Not anything.

CASEY. A lot of things. He's gifted.

ERIC. Well it's very nice.

CASEY. He's a wonderful writer too. He writes the most brilliant poems.

ALAN. That's – unusual for a man.

BRETT. You're embarrassing me, Casey.

ALAN. You're embarrassing yourself, Brett.

    ALAN *laughs, picks up some food.*

CYNTHIA. So a writer and a cook?

CASEY. And a landscape gardener.

BRETT. That's just the day job.

ERIC. God.

CASEY. He's great with nature.

ERIC. I'm feeling a bit – insecure now.

CASEY. And his favourite film's *Gone with the Wind*! How sexy is that. For a landscape gardener.

PAULINE. And you're a poet?

BRETT. No, she's making it sound – I'm not really a poet. I just dabble.

CASEY. You should read some of them.

    PAULINE *looks at* ALAN *witheringly.*

PAULINE. I could have done with a bit more poetry in my life, couldn't I, girls?

ALAN *rolls his eyes.* CASEY *continues.*

CASEY. He wrote this one line –

BRETT (*embarrassed*). Casey…

CASEY. About my heart. (*Reciting.*) 'As big and kind as the moon.'

She looks at them, thrilled.

Isn't that fabulous? He just made that up!

BRETT *steps in to explain.*

BRETT. Well it's sort of out of context now but basically the line goes… 'You have the face of an ageless warrior queen, but a heart' –

ALAN. Arse?

CASEY. Heart!

BRETT.…as big and kind as the moon.

BRETT *and* CASEY *look at one another lovingly.*

ALAN. And you made that up yourself, Brett?

BRETT. Yes.

CASEY. Isn't he incredible?

ERIC. Unbelievable.

CASEY. Didn't I tell you?

CYNTHIA. You did. You – did.

CYNTHIA *looks at him, trying to gauge.*

So how did you meet again?

CASEY *smiles, about to launch in to the story.*

CASEY. Well.

CYNTHIA. Which app?

CASEY *stops.*

CASEY. What?

CYNTHIA. Which dating app?

CASEY *looks at* BRETT, *embarrassed.*

CASEY. We didn't meet on a dating app.

CYNTHIA. Casey.

CASEY. We didn't.

ERIC. It's nothing to be ashamed of. Normal people are doing it now.

CASEY (*annoyed*). But we didn't!

CYNTHIA. Okay. Fine. Where *did* you meet then?

CASEY. We met… on a bus actually.

ALAN. A bus?

CASEY. Yeah.

CYNTHIA. Which bus?

CASEY. The bus from town to Dún Laoghaire.

ALAN. The 7?

CASEY. I don't remember the number.

CYNTHIA. The 45?

CASEY. One of them.

PAULINE. And what were you doing out in Dún Laoghaire?

CASEY. Well that's the extraordinary thing…

She looks at BRETT, *smiles.*

…I went to see the sea.

BRETT *smiles back.*

BRETT. It's kind of a romantic story, isn't it, Casey?

CASEY. Kind of.

They look at one another lovingly.

BRETT. Do you want to tell it?

CASEY *shakes her head.*

CASEY. No you tell it.

BRETT. Casey tells it better than me.

CASEY. No, he tells it better than me.

They canoodle into one another. Stroking faces, being all lovey-dovey.

BRETT. But you're good at all the detail.

CASEY. I prefer your accent.

BRETT. I prefer *your* accent.

CASEY. Oh baby.

BRETT. Oh baby.

ALAN. Ah here –

CYNTHIA. Will one of you tell bloody the story?

BRETT. Well. Okay… sure. So it was a Tuesday. Beautiful. Crisp January Tuesday and I was sort of –

CASEY (*feeding him*). New in town.

BRETT. Yeah I was new in town and I wanted to do something… different. Not touristy.

ALAN. You're not from round here, are you not, Brett?

PAULINE. Sure of course he's not. Look at the lovely grand build of him. Men round here don't look like that.

ERIC. Don't they?

ERIC *looks at himself, a bit uncertain.*

CYNTHIA. And the accent.

ALAN. What accent?

PAULINE. He's clearly American.

ALAN. Are you?

BRETT. Well yes as it happens.

ERIC. Which part?

BRETT. All over really.

ALAN. And how tall would you be now, Brett?

BRETT. Tall?

ALAN. Ballpark.

BRETT. About six-two.

CYNTHIA. Will you just let him tell the bloody story – go on, Brett.

BRETT. So yeah – um I wanted to do something different. And someone said there's this Viking boat which does these tours and people wear hats.

CYNTHIA. So you weren't being touristy –

BRETT. It's just I love boats and I think Vikings are awesome so I thought I'd –

ERIC. Give it a shot.

BRETT. So I was wandering around looking for this bus. And I was standing at the bus stop in Nassau Street.

CASEY. The wrong bus stop in Nassau Street might I add.

CASEY and BRETT laugh at this mix-up.

BRETT. And I'm trying to get to grips with this map that's not making any sense and I look up and suddenly I'm just stopped in my tracks by this… vision.

CASEY smiles.

The family look at her, clearly somewhat bewildered by this description.

PAULINE. … You mean Casey?

BRETT. Yes. Casey. She was – she was leaning against the wall, reading a book. And she was so engrossed, she didn't even see me. But I saw her, my god… and it was like, well, I don't want to get too –

CASEY. No.

BRETT. But I did say to you afterwards –

CASEY. I know!

BRETT. That it was like –

CASEY (*excitedly*). Being hit by lightning.

She looks around, pleased with herself.

ERIC. Ouch.

BRETT. In a good way. But of course I didn't know who she was. And you can't just walk up to someone you've never met who's reading a book.

PAULINE. No.

BRETT. But then she looked up. And she looked right at me. And she smiled. And that smile… I swear to god…

BRETT and CASEY *share a personal moment of being lost in each other.*

CYNTHIA. So what happened then?

BRETT. I followed her onto the bus.

CYNTHIA. You – followed her onto the bus?

ERIC. So you ditched the Viking thing, did you?

BRETT. I couldn't help myself.

CYNTHIA. You couldn't help yourself following her onto a bus?

BRETT. I was captivated.

CYNTHIA. Okay.

BRETT. I was sitting at the front. I kept having to turn around.

CASEY *and* BRETT *smile at each other.*

CYNTHIA. And this was fine with you?

CASEY. What do you mean?

CYNTHIA. This strange man turning around and staring at you on the bus?

CASEY. Well… Yeah.

CYNTHIA. Okay.

CASEY. What?

CYNTHIA. Nothing. Go on.

CASEY. Well I tried not to stare back.

CASEY *and* BRETT *smile at each other, flirting. They will do this throughout.*

BRETT. But you wanted to stare back.

CASEY. I *might* have wanted to stare back… I kept looking at his shoulders.

And I kept tracing the outline of his muscles in my mind under his clothes and I kept getting this feeling.

ALAN. Okay /

CASEY. This really strong overwhelming feeling near my stomach /

ALAN. I think we get the idea /

CASEY. Like I wanted to touch him.

ALAN. Yep /

CASEY. I wanted to run my hands all over him, like all over his entire body – even his heart and his liver and his pancreas if I could –

ALAN. I'll have another drop of this.

CASEY. So I get off the bus.

BRETT. And I get off the bus.

CASEY. And I'm trying not to look at him.

BRETT. And I'm *totally* looking at her. And I'm thinking, I've got this shot, you know, I've got this one shot to talk to this beautiful girl and if I don't take it

CASEY. And I'm standing by the traffic lights /

BRETT. And I'm looking at her thinking. She's about to cross that road. She's about to walk across that road and out of my life /

CASEY. And the little man turns green. And I'm taking a step forward /

BRETT. And I see her taking a step forward and I imagine her disappearing into the crowd and without even thinking I just sort of rush at her.

He takes CASEY *by the arm dramatically.*

PAULINE *gasps* –

PAULINE. Oh.

BRETT. And I say – I say – this is going to sound a bit strange and you might even think it's a little creepy but you have the most beautiful eyes I think I've ever seen.

PAULINE. Ah, god.

CYNTHIA. And what did you say to that?

BRETT. She blushed.

CASEY. I blushed.

BRETT. And then I kissed her.

CYNTHIA. What!

CASEY. He did!

PAULINE. You kissed her?

ERIC. With tongues?

CASEY. With everything. Right there in the middle of the street. Without even asking me my name.

BRETT. It was kind of scary – the way it just took me over.

CYNTHIA. Yes.

BRETT. But I had to do it. I had no choice. Because I knew.

CASEY. We both knew.

PAULINE. You knew what?

They look at one another.

CASEY.…That we were in love.

A silence.

The whole room stares at them.

ALAN. And had either of you a drink taken?

CASEY. Dad!

ALAN. It's a perfectly legitimate question.

CASEY. It's our story. It's how we met.

PAULINE. Well, it sounds very intense.

CASEY. It *was* very intense.

ERIC. I think it's great. You can tell a lot about a relationship from how people meet.

PAULINE. Well ye've a great story. Cynthia and Eric have a great story.

CASEY *visibly deflates*.

CYNTHIA. No we don't.

ERIC. Yes we do.

CASEY. Well we've heard that story before.

PAULINE. Eric gave Cynthia her big break in television.

BRETT *looks at* CYNTHIA.

BRETT. Television. Right! I thought I recognised you.

CYNTHIA. Really?

CASEY. Really?

BRETT. Yeah. The moment I walked in the door I thought I know her from somewhere. You do that little slot, don't you? The one after the news – what's it called – *Whatever the Weather*.

CYNTHIA. Yes.

PAULINE. That's it!

BRETT. God I love that show.

CYNTHIA. Really?

PAULINE. Cynthia invented that show.

CYNTHIA. Mom.

BRETT. You invented it?

CYNTHIA (*faux-modesty*). It was just my idea.

BRETT. It's a great idea. Mixing philosophy and weather. It's such a quirky little slot – or what would you call it?

CASEY. A little slot.

CYNTHIA. Actually they call it a show.

CASEY. Do they?

CYNTHIA. Yes.

CASEY. But it's only five minutes long.

CYNTHIA. Well a show is a show, Casey.

CASEY. It just doesn't seem like a proper show.

ERIC. That's what I say about most of what's on these days. How the fuck did this get commissioned when there are people out here with genuinely original ideas who can't get a look-in. What the hell is that about, you know?

ALAN. Hmmn.

Everyone's at a bit of a loss.

BRETT. Wow. You never said you had a famous sister, Casey.

CASEY. You never said you – liked that show.

PAULINE (*to* BRETT). Well, it's hard on her.

CASEY. What?

PAULINE. Having a famous sister.

CASEY. No it's not.

PAULINE. They were very different growing up. Cynthia was the sporty outgoing one and Casey was the helper. But we always made an effort to treat them exactly the same, didn't we, Alan? Down to the shoes on their feet. Exactly the same. Alan and I met at dance hall.

ALAN. What?

PAULINE. Since we're telling stories.

ALAN. We're not telling stories.

PAULINE. He was doing a line with someone else at the time but couldn't take his eyes off me.

ALAN. Let's not get into this.

PAULINE. Should've known then, shouldn't I. Never bite a snake cos you'll be bitten yourself – isn't that the saying, Brett?

BRETT. I don't actually know that saying, Mrs Cassidy.

ALAN. Cos she made it up. We're not here to talk about that, Pauline. We're here to have a nice dinner and be civil and meet Casey's new fella. So where are you living then, Brett?

BRETT. Living?

ALAN. While you're in town.

BRETT. Oh.

He looks at CASEY, *smiles*.

Well I'm... living here.

ALAN. Where?

BRETT. Here.

ALAN. Here, here?

CYNTHIA. With Casey?

CASEY. Yes.

PAULINE.... When did you move in?

CASEY. The day after we met.

CYNTHIA. Which was when exactly?

CASEY. Two weeks ago last Tuesday.

PAULINE. Casey.

CASEY. You haven't heard the best part yet – Brett and I are getting married!

ALAN. What?

CASEY beams.

CASEY. He proposed!

She squeals.

Isn't that exciting?

CYNTHIA. You can't be serious.

CASEY. Why not?

CYNTHIA. Because you met on a bus.

CASEY. What does that matter?

CYNTHIA. Two weeks ago.

PAULINE. Casey...

CASEY. We're in love.

BRETT. We are. Very much so.

> *He kisses her, tender. They look at the family.*
>
> *Silence.*

ALAN. Ah she's pulling our leg.

CASEY (*hurt*). What does that mean?

PAULINE. That isn't something you joke about, Casey.

CASEY. I'm not joking.

ALAN. Don't be ridiculous.

CASEY. We are getting married.

CYNTHIA. You don't even know him.

ALAN. Do you think we came down in the last shower?

CASEY. But it's true.

ALAN. Jaysus, you had us going there for a minute though.

CASEY. We are getting married. We're getting married – WE'RE GETTING MARRIED. Why is that so hard to believe?

PAULINE. Because it seems a bit –

CYNTHIA. Mental.

PAULINE. Rushed. It seems a bit rushed. It seems a bit – impulsive.

CASEY. Well we're not getting married *right now*.

BRETT. No, god no. Not – right now.

CASEY. We're going to wait at least a month.

ALAN. A month!

BRETT. We haven't settled on a date.

CASEY. But it'll probably be the twenty-fifth.

ALAN. The twenty-fifth next month?

PAULINE. Casey, we're not trying to… but there are things to… what about your health?

> CASEY *looks at* BRETT, *suddenly self-conscious.*

CASEY. What about my health?

PAULINE. You know you have to mind yourself.

CASEY. I'm fine.

ALAN. I didn't even kiss your mother for three whole months.

CASEY. And look how that turned out.

BRETT. Maybe I should have asked for your permission, Mr Cassidy?

ALAN. Permission?

BRETT. For Casey's hand?

ALAN. No, god. I don't want to be involved.

CASEY. Thanks.

CYNTHIA. We're not trying to offend you, Brett. We're really not. It's just.

BRETT. No. I get it. You're family. You're – worried. I mean you don't even know me. I'm sure when my folks hear, they'll be a little… it *is* kind of a whirlwind but it just… felt right. Didn't it, Casey?

CASEY. Yes. It did.

BRETT. It just felt… natural.

PAULINE. Well I'm sure it did, but Casey can be a bit –

CASEY *becomes angry.*

CASEY. I'm not being a bit anything. We're not rushing into anything. We've thought about this very carefully, haven't we, Brett?

BRETT. We have, we really have.

CASEY. We've fallen in love. And we're getting married and yes, it's been fast and yes, it's been a whirlwind but that's – just the way it is.

BRETT *puts his arm around* CASEY.

They look at the family, a firm show of togetherness.

Sometimes… you just know.

They smile.

Two

An office.

Two chairs facing one another like a therapist's office.

CASEY *is sitting in one of them.* TESS *is opposite her writing things in a notepad.*

TESS. So it's your sister again?

CASEY. Yes. Well no.

TESS. But she *is* usually the source of your –

CASEY. She is usually. But this time it was all of them really. My whole family. I introduced them to Brett.

TESS. Ah.

   TESS *writes this down in her notepad.*

CASEY. And they questioned my health.

TESS. What day was this?

CASEY.…Tuesday I think?

   TESS *writes this down.*

TESS. Tuesday. (*Writing.*) Family drama…

CASEY (*agitated*). Like the first thing they did when we said we're getting married was bring up my condition. Not 'congratulations, that's wonderful, Casey, we're so happy you've met someone…'

   CASEY *looks at* TESS *for some emotional back-up.*

TESS. And how is your condition?

CASEY. Hmmn?

   This isn't the response she wanted.

TESS. You're still taking medication?

   CASEY *seems uncomfortable.*

CASEY. Well – yeah. But like a really low dosage. Most dentists are on more antidepressants than me.

   CASEY *laughs.*

   TESS *stares at her, stone-faced.*

TESS. What did we say about using humour as a deflection, Casey?

CASEY *stops*.

CASEY. …Sorry. I'm managing it.

TESS *writes something down*.

TESS. We just have to be cautious. You would tell me if there was any –

CASEY. I've been doing really well. Been getting up early, I've found a second job… everything's been – great.

TESS *smiles*.

TESS. Well that's great.

CASEY. So my family should be happy for me?

TESS. Ah ah – no shoulds.

CASEY. But I was so excited and Brett was so gorgeous –

TESS. Which is wonderful.

CASEY. They didn't think so. It's like they have me in a box.

TESS. No one can put you in a box you don't want to be in.

CASEY. Well they put me in a hospital once so –

TESS. Let's not go down negativity junction.

CASEY. Sorry.

TESS. Let's focus on the present and build on that. Things are going well with Brett…

CASEY. Things are going great with Brett.

TESS *smiles, writes it down*.

TESS. Things are better than they were.

CASEY. Yes they are. They definitely – are.

TESS *keeps writing*.

TESS. He's everything you've wanted in a partner.

CASEY. I can't believe it!

TESS. You're living the life of your dreams.

CASEY. Well in the life of my dreams, I'd look like Audrey Hepburn and the clouds'd be made of marshmallows and you could eat them without getting fat –

CASEY *sees* TESS*'s face and pulls back.*

...but yeah, close.

TESS. Nothing we can do about the clouds, Casey.

CASEY. No I know –

TESS. But your internal narrative...

CASEY. I just wish – sometimes they could be a bit – happier for me. You know? My family.

TESS. Hmmn.

CASEY (*quickly*). I mean I know happiness comes from within.

TESS *writes something down.*

TESS. Not necessarily.

CASEY. But I should... find it in myself?

TESS. Perhaps. (*Then.*) Or perhaps you just need to work a bit harder? To make them see what you've got.

CASEY *seems a bit uncertain.*

CASEY....Right.

CASEY *thinks for a beat.*

So...

TESS *glances at the clock on her desk.*

TESS. I'm afraid we're out of time.

CASEY. Oh.

TESS. I've made some notes.

Three

A doorbell. CASEY*'s flat. Afternoon.*

CYNTHIA *stands with a plant.*

CYNTHIA. I brought you a plant.

CASEY. Oh.

CYNTHIA. For the flat.

CASEY. Right.

CASEY *takes the plant, looks at it.*

CYNTHIA. Brett will know what it is.

CASEY. Great. Thanks.

CYNTHIA. Are you going somewhere?

CASEY. No.

CYNTHIA. You look dressed up.

CASEY. Do I?

CYNTHIA. You look like you're off to a wedding.

CASEY. We're just staying in.

CYNTHIA. It's kind of a fancy hat for just staying in.

CASEY. Well we're going to have tea. On the veranda.

CYNTHIA. When did you get a veranda?

CASEY. We just say that. It's sort of a thing we say now. Tea on the veranda. Like date night.

CYNTHIA. Okay.

Beat.

So where do you actually have the tea?

CASEY. Living room.

Beat.

Do you want to… come in?

CYNTHIA. Well, I don't want to impose.

CASEY. Okay, thanks for the plant.

CASEY *moves to close the door.*

CYNTHIA. Unless you… want me to –

CASEY. No we're happy.

CYNTHIA. Just… well because I just – kind of wanted to say sorry.

CASEY *looks at her.*

CASEY. For what?

CYNTHIA. For the other day. I thought we might have upset you.

CASEY. No.

CYNTHIA. Oh good.

CASEY. But you were rude to Brett.

CYNTHIA. I don't think we were rude to Brett.

CASEY. I thought you were very rude to Brett.

CYNTHIA. Well, maybe we weren't as enthusiastic as you had – hoped. But I'm sure you understand under the circumstances –

CASEY. What circumstances?

CYNTHIA. Casey…

BRETT *arrives holding a tea towel.*

BRETT. Casey, tea's ready. Cynthia! What a nice surprise.

CYNTHIA. Hi – Brett. You're wearing an apron.

CASEY. Cynthia came to apologise to you.

BRETT. To me? What for?

CYNTHIA *opens her mouth.*

CASEY. For being rude the other day.

BRETT. You weren't rude.

CASEY. She feels very bad about it.

BRETT. Don't be silly.

CASEY. She brought us a plant.

BRETT. Well that is so… thank you.

CYNTHIA. I said you'd know what it is.

He looks at it.

BRETT. Yes… yeah.

CYNTHIA. I don't remember the name.

BRETT. Well, there are so many… We'll put it in the garden.

CYNTHIA. Oh cos he told me in the shop it's an indoor species.

BRETT. Huh.

CYNTHIA. But maybe it can go in the garden. He just said it… thrives in darkness.

BRETT. No plant thrives in darkness.

CYNTHIA. Oh.

BRETT. I'm pretty sure they need light to stay alive.

CYNTHIA. It's just what the man said.

CASEY. Brett knows what he's talking about, Cynthia.

CYNTHIA. I know.

CASEY. You can see his expertise.

BRETT *smiles at* CYNTHIA.

BRETT. …I think he might have been teasing you.

CYNTHIA. Well now I feel stupid.

BRETT. Don't feel stupid. Why don't you stay for tea?

CASEY. She can't.

BRETT. That's a shame. I made scones.

CYNTHIA. Scones?

CASEY. She's very busy.

BRETT. Of course – the show.

CYNTHIA. Yes. We're planning next week's episodes. Wittgenstein and Rorty. And Eric has a big pitch about his – orphans thing… the wife of an unemployed producer's work is never done.

She laughs, a little brittle. BRETT *smiles at her.*

BRETT. He's lucky you're so supportive.

CYNTHIA. Well.

CASEY *looks at* BRETT, *gets in quickly.*

CASEY. I'm lucky *you're* so supportive. He did everything this afternoon – even baked the scones.

CYNTHIA. I heard.

CASEY. You know sometimes he doesn't even let me pour the tea. He literally snatches the teapot out of my hand.

CYNTHIA. Really?

CASEY. In a nice way.

BRETT *looks a little embarrassed.*

BRETT. I just like to spoil her.

CYNTHIA *looks at them, bewildered.*

CASEY. He's taking me for a walk later. A surprise romantic tour of the city.

CYNTHIA. A surprise romantic tour of the city?… On a Monday?

BRETT. I think it's important to find the unusual in the – everyday, you know.

CYNTHIA. I guess.

BRETT. Otherwise we lose perspective and don't see the beauty that's right in front of us.

He holds CYNTHIA'*s gaze for a moment too long.*

A beat.

CASEY *anxiously grabs his arm.*

CASEY. You're amazing.

He turns to CASEY.

BRETT. No *you're* amazing.

They start to nuzzle. CYNTHIA *watches, uncomfortable.*

CYNTHIA. You know, I think I'll leave you to it. I should be – getting home.

   BRETT *breaks away.*

BRETT. You sure you can't stay?

CYNTHIA. No, I've got to – I've never been one for verandas.

BRETT. Right. Well… Thank you for the plant.

CASEY. Yeah. Thanks, Cynthia.

CYNTHIA.…Pleasure.

   CASEY *and* BRETT *go inside.*

   CYNTHIA *is left on the doorstep feeling strange.*

Four

A slide:

'Brett and Casey's romantic walk in the city.'

Music.

The following is suggestive rather than absolute – the idea is that the walk should be iconic and free-flowing and perfectly choreographed like an old-fashioned Hollywood silent movie.

BRETT *is holding* CASEY's *hand as he shows her the city's sights. Dublin glittering romantically behind them – lights, water, the Ha'penny Bridge –* CASEY *is laughing and snuggling under his arm.*

People walk by and smile at them in recognition at what it is like to be young and in love.

BRETT *jumps up on the side of the fountain and splashes some water at* CASEY.

CASEY *jumps up too and splashes some water back.*

BRETT *pretends he might fall in.* CASEY *pulls him back.*

A woman with a candyfloss machine appears, hands them a large pink roll of floss.

BRETT *tries to pay, but the woman waves him off and walks away.*

BRETT *holds the candyfloss up and both he and* CASEY *take a bite at the same time.*

A girl walking a small cute dog passes.

CASEY *bends down and picks the dog up. She and* BRETT *coo over it. The girl nods approvingly.*

A three-piece mariachi band strike up and play something romantic.

BRETT *pulls* CASEY *away from the dog and implies that they should dance.*

CASEY *shakes her head – indicating she's shy.*

A man in a long raincoat – SEBASTIAN *– walks on and watches the band.*

BRETT, *aware of* SEBASTIAN, *tries to coax* CASEY *to dance again.*

CASEY *shakes her head, embarrassed.*

BRETT *hands* SEBASTIAN *the candyfloss while* CASEY *looks the other way.*

Almost imperceptibly SEBASTIAN *deposits the candyfloss in the bin.*

BRETT *grabs* CASEY *more determinedly and begins to dance with her.*

This time she gives in and follows.

BRETT *is dazzling in the lead.*

CASEY*'s better than we expect.*

At the finale, BRETT *picks* CASEY *up and dips her dramatically.*

He and CASEY *kiss.*

SEBASTIAN *opens his raincoat and takes out a single red rose.*

As BRETT *kisses* CASEY, *he opens one eye and takes the rose from* SEBASTIAN.

SEBASTIAN *swiftly leaves the stage.*

BRETT *gives* CASEY *the rose.*

She smells it and looks at him as if to say 'It's beautiful.'

Then in a rush of love and excitement they run up and onto the bridge. The fountain starts to spout joyously – spraying water as CASEY *and* BRETT *stand on the bridge, look out at the city and its twinkling lights and wallow in the wonder of their love.*

If birds could fly from trees and land on their shoulders, they would…

Very slow fade to –

Five

The sound of a telephone ringing.

Lights up on what will be a three-way phone conversation.

ALAN. Hello?

PAULINE. Hi.

ALAN. Oh hi.

PAULINE. Is Barbara there?

ALAN. Why do you want to speak to Barbara?

PAULINE. I don't want to speak to her, I'm just asking if she's there.

ALAN. What are you calling for, Pauline?

PAULINE. I'm worried about Casey.

ALAN. Oh.

PAULINE. Aren't you?

ALAN. I don't know.

PAULINE. Do you think he means it, this Brett character?

ALAN. Means what?

PAULINE. That he's going to marry her. Or do you think he's leading her up the garden path?

ALAN. Well I suppose he is a landscape –

PAULINE. Don't, Alan, I'm not in the mood.

ALAN. Well I'm not in the mood to pay for two weddings in the space of five years.

PAULINE. I don't think you'll have to pay for it.

ALAN. Why not?

PAULINE. She's got some sort of package. All-inclusive. She told me last night she's working two jobs.

ALAN. Two?

PAULINE. They must be saving up.

ALAN. Well that's something. She always had a very good work ethic, Casey. An excellent trait in a woman.

PAULINE. How do you think she seemed though the other night?

ALAN. She seems fine.

PAULINE. We have to keep an eye on her.

The sound of ringing.

Oh god the other line's going. Hang on a sec – Hello?

CYNTHIA. Mom?

PAULINE. Yes dear.

CYNTHIA. I'm worried about Casey.

PAULINE. I'm just on the phone to your father. He's worried about her too.

CYNTHIA. I think Brett might be a gigolo.

PAULINE. What?

CYNTHIA. Or a con man. There's no other way to explain it.

PAULINE. Hang on a second. Alan, are you there?

ALAN. Course I am.

PAULINE. Cynthia's on the other line. She thinks Brett's
   a prostitute.

ALAN. What?

PAULINE. A prostitute.

ALAN. But he's six-foot-two.

PAULINE. Hang on a second. Cynthia?

CYNTHIA. Yeah.

PAULINE. Your father thinks he's too tall.

CYNTHIA. Something's not right about it. I called round
   yesterday and they were all over each other. It was disgusting.

PAULINE. Well now we don't want to jump to conclusions –

CYNTHIA. And the way he's moved in like that and behaves
   all devoted and mesmerised by her –

PAULINE. Well /

CYNTHIA. This is Casey we're talking about. You know she's
   working two jobs now?

PAULINE. They're saving for the wedding.

CYNTHIA. There won't be a wedding. The man's a thief and
   he's exploiting her.

PAULINE. I thought you said he was a prostitute.

CYNTHIA. He could be both. Con men often are.

PAULINE. Oh god. Hang on. Alan?

ALAN. Is the landscape gardener a code do you think?

PAULINE. What?

ALAN. You know – trimming bushes?

PAULINE. Cynthia thinks he's a thief. Possibly a con man. And
   a lot of them are also prostitutes.

ALAN. Jesus.

PAULINE. I know.

ALAN. We're out of our depth.

PAULINE. He seemed like such a nice fellow.

CYNTHIA. They always do.

PAULINE. Oh I hit the wrong button. (*To* ALAN.) He seemed like such a nice fellow.

ALAN. They often do.

PAULINE. This is so unfortunate.

ALAN. Hmmn.

PAULINE. When she said she'd met someone my heart lifted. It's not easy at her age.

ALAN. It's not easy at any age.

PAULINE. It wasn't a problem for you.

ALAN. Ah here.

PAULINE. And with her condition.

ALAN. I know.

PAULINE. It's desperate.

ALAN. If we're right.

PAULINE. What?

ALAN. Well, we could be making assumptions.

PAULINE. Cynthia says they couldn't keep their hands off each other.

ALAN. Sure isn't that what lovers do?

PAULINE. I don't know, Alan. Is that what lovers do?

ALAN. I'm just saying it's not abnormal. I mean is there any possibility…

PAULINE. What?

ALAN. That he could just be a nice fellow and we're not being fair?

PAULINE *thinks*.

PAULINE. I'll ask Cynthia. Your father wants to know is there any possibility that he could just be a nice fellow and we're not being fair?

CYNTHIA. What does that mean?

PAULINE. I'll ask him. She wants to know what that means?

ALAN. I mean is there any possibility that he could just like her and want to marry her and it's as simple as that?

PAULINE. Hang on. Is there any possibility that he could just like her and want to marry her and it's as simple as that?

CYNTHIA. I'm not following.

PAULINE. She's not following, Alan. Be more specific.

ALAN. I *mean…* is there any possibility it's just true?

They stop and mull this.

Six

CYNTHIA *on television, wearing bright colours.*

CYNTHIA (*presenting*). It's raining it's pouring, the whole country's roaring –

'When are we going to see the sun again?'

BRETT *comes on and watches her.*

Well I have a question for you. How do we know we ever saw it in the first place? How do we know that the sun even exists?

The eighteenth-century philosopher Bishop George Berkeley said reality is governed by perception. Omne esse est percipi – 'to be, is to be perceived'. So we see a plate – we know it exists. But if we put that same plate in a cupboard and close the door, how do we know that the plate is still here? And could it be the same with the –

She goes dark suddenly.

BRETT *looks around.*

CASEY *stands with the remote.*

CASEY. Sorry. Did you want to watch that?

BRETT. No. It was just – on when I came in.

He starts to busy himself.

CASEY. I can turn it back. You said you were a fan.

BRETT. I was being nice. You look pretty.

CASEY. *She* looks pretty. She always looks pretty on the telly.

BRETT *shrugs*.

BRETT. I hadn't noticed.

CASEY. She doesn't know anything about philosophy, you know. I mean she did arts. But she's no real feeling… half of what she says she doesn't understand.

BRETT. They must have researchers.

CASEY. It's because she's beautiful. That's why people watch it. People used to stare at her long before she was famous. They've done it since she was a little girl. It's mad how people pay attention if you're pretty. They want to be around you all the time. You don't even have to do anything. It's like she's – magic or something.

BRETT. I really hadn't noticed.

CASEY. Everyone notices.

BRETT *tries to think of something to say.*

BRETT. Well she's not a patch on you.

This doesn't seem to have the desired effect.

CASEY. I just came to say goodbye. I'm working tonight. You probably won't be here when I get back.

BRETT. No.

CASEY. So, when will I…

BRETT. Thursday.

CASEY. Okay. Thursday. I'll look forward to that.

She looks at him, sadly.

BRETT.…Are you okay?

CASEY. Me? Yeah.

BRETT. You seem kind of sad.

CASEY. No.

BRETT. You look a little sad.

CASEY. No.

Beat.

…It's lonely when you're gone.

BRETT. I think of you every day.

She nods, unconvinced.

I think of you every night.

CASEY. I think of you too.

Beat.

Do you ever think sometimes… if you could just change one little thing about yourself, everything would be okay?

BRETT *looks confused.*

BRETT.…What do you mean?

CASEY. Do you ever – do you ever feel like you're on the outside of a big party, looking in? Or maybe – maybe you've been invited to the party, but you don't really feel like you belong there. Not really. Cos – no one's really listening to your stories, and they don't quite get your jokes and no matter what you do, no matter how hard you try – to laugh or fit in and *look* like you're doing the same things they're doing – it doesn't make any difference. You just don't have the magic ingredient. And nothing you can do will ever change it.

She looks at him, hopeful.

…Do you ever feel like that?

BRETT. Um…Well… do you want me to…

He's clearly at a loss.

CASEY. It doesn't matter. Forget it. I'm being stupid.

BRETT *looks uncomfortable.*

BRETT. I'm not saying the right thing, am I? I'm not doing the right –

He seems to struggle.

CASEY. I should go.

BRETT. No hang on. I'll get there.

CASEY. No, it's fine, really. I'm being silly. See you Thursday.

BRETT. Wait. Casey –

Suddenly –

Have you ever been to Paris?

She stops, looks at him, surprised.

CASEY. Paris?

BRETT. Yeah. Have you ever been?

CASEY.…No.

BRETT. We should go. Why don't we go? This weekend, you and me.

CASEY. To Paris?

CASEY *seems to light up.*

BRETT. You have to see Paris. Paris is something you have to see. I want to take you.

CASEY. Really?

BRETT. I want to walk with you by Notre-Dame. I want to show you the Seine at night. I want to picnic in the Tuileries Garden and make love to you in the Louvre.

CASEY *laughs. He takes her hand.*

CASEY. In the Louvre?

BRETT. Okay not *in* the Louvre, but we should go to the Louvre. Early before it gets too crowded.

CASEY. I've always wanted to go to Paris.

BRETT. Well let's do it. Let's go. Let's be spontaneous.

CASEY.…Okay.

BRETT. Okay!

CASEY. Let's go to Paris!

BRETT. Great!… I mean – you can afford it, right?

CASEY. Oh.

BRETT. Cos I don't want to put you – us – under any kind of strain.

CASEY. No… no, I can afford it.

BRETT. You sure?

CASEY. Yes. Yeah. We can afford it.

BRETT. Really?

CASEY. I'll find a way to pay.

BRETT. Great. That's. Great. I can't wait.

CASEY. Me neither.

He looks at her, intense.

BRETT. I love you.

She smiles, picks up her work bag.

CASEY. Frankly my dear I don't give a damn.

She moves to the door, then turns back, deeply serious.

That isn't true, by the way.

He nods. She leaves. A silence.

He picks up the remote and turns on the television.
CYNTHIA *reappears.*

CYNTHIA. So if Mr Berkeley is correct, we can just *perceive* that the sun is out, it's ninety degrees and it's time to hit the beach.

She mock-shivers.

But maybe take that umbrella… just in case.

She smiles.

It goes black.

Seven

An office.

SEBASTIAN *at a desk.*

Two chairs facing one another as before. Like a therapy session.

SEBASTIAN *presses a button on some sort of intercom.* TESS*'s voice answers.*

SEBASTIAN. Tess, it's ten-past.

TESS. I'm not the PA, Sebastian.

SEBASTIAN. Well who's in charge of the diary? I should have a three o'clock.

The door opens. BRETT *comes in, sort of breathless.*

BRETT. Hey.

SEBASTIAN. Forget it. He's here.

BRETT. Sorry to keep you, I was – coming from Casey's. Don't quite have a handle on the route –

SEBASTIAN. Oh you're doing the… [accent.]

BRETT. Yeah I thought I should /

SEBASTIAN. Excellent, very good. Have a seat.

   BRETT *sits.*

   We won't have time for the full hour.

BRETT. That's okay. I just wanted to –

   SEBASTIAN *holds a hand up as if to stop him.*

SEBASTIAN. Ap!

   BRETT *looks confused.*

BRETT.…Sorry?

SEBASTIAN. Let's just slow it down, shall we.

BRETT. Oh.

SEBASTIAN. Come into the room.

SEBASTIAN *takes a breath, looking at* BRETT, *signalling he should copy.*

BRETT *copies, watching him closely.*

SEBASTIAN *exhales deeply.* BRETT *exhales deeply.*

And again.

They do it again.

SEBASTIAN *smiles.*

So. How have you been – Brett?

BRETT. Really well.

SEBASTIAN. How is everything going with…

SEBASTIAN *searches through his notes.*

BRETT.…Casey.

SEBASTIAN. Yes, Casey.

BRETT. Really good. We're going to Paris tonight.

SEBASTIAN. Ah.

BRETT. A mini-break. I suggested it. (*Anxious.*) Do you think that's okay?

SEBASTIAN. Nothing wrong with a little spontaneity.

BRETT (*relieved*). Oh good. I don't want to be presumptuous but – she seemed pleased.

SEBASTIAN *takes out a pen, starts to write things down.*

SEBASTIAN. And how does that make you feel?

BRETT. Good. I mean god – you know, it's great to see her so happy. Cos I want this to work.

SEBASTIAN. Course you do.

BRETT. No, I really – I'm in this, for the long haul you know.

SEBASTIAN. You're committed?

BRETT. Yes, I'm committed. Totally.

SEBASTIAN. So you're still planning on going ahead with the –

BRETT. Absolutely.

SEBASTIAN. Because it's not a decision to be taken lightly?

BRETT. I know that. And I'm not. I want this. I'm ready. I mean I know I've had my issues with –

SEBASTIAN. Hmm.

BRETT. But this time I'm ready to –

SEBASTIAN. Make the leap.

BRETT. Yes!

SEBASTIAN. Well that is wonderful to hear. *That's* what our work has been about.

    BRETT *smiles. Then stops smiling.*

BRETT. It's just…

SEBASTIAN.… Yes?

BRETT. Well sometimes…

SEBASTIAN. Yes?

BRETT. I mean everything's going well with Casey and we're happy and all, but sometimes I've noticed, it can feel a little… forced.

SEBASTIAN. Forced?

    SEBASTIAN *writes this down.*

BRETT. Just sometimes.

SEBASTIAN. What do you mean by forced?

BRETT. Well sometimes I don't know what to say to her. Like she's telling me something – something sensitive or deeply personal to her – and I literally cannot think of a single thing to say… Not one thing.

SEBASTIAN. That's perfectly normal.

BRETT. Is it?

SEBASTIAN. Course.

BRETT. In a healthy relationship?

SEBASTIAN. Some of the healthiest relationships are founded in silence.

BRETT. I just worry that it's something I'm doing.

SEBASTIAN. It's not.

BRETT. But maybe there's something I could be doing differently? You must have tips. With all your –

SEBASTIAN. We're not here to talk about me.

BRETT. But given my history –

SEBASTIAN. That's in the past.

BRETT. But at the same time –

SEBASTIAN. You're very different now. Look at you.

BRETT *looks at himself*.

BRETT. I just worry if I get frustrated or bored or, god forbid – angry I could end up making the same –

SEBASTIAN. Brett /

BRETT. – or doing something really –

SEBASTIAN (*forceful*). Brett.

BRETT *stops*.

We mustn't let the past dictate the future. Whatever you did back then was back then. You're not that boy any more.

BRETT. I know.

SEBASTIAN. You're – Brett.

BRETT *nods, but he still seems anxious*.

BRETT. So it shouldn't feel… easier?

SEBASTIAN *suddenly slams his hand down*.

SEBASTIAN. And that right there is the problem with Western ideology! The Buddhists believe life is suffering.

BRETT....Okay.

SEBASTIAN. Suffering being our resistance to impermanence.
    But impermanence being the essence of life!

    BRETT *is trying to understand*.

BRETT. Right…

SEBASTIAN. Right?

    BRETT *nods, but is struggling*.

BRETT....I just want to be – good. A good person. You know?

SEBASTIAN. Listen if anything too challenging comes up, you
    can always call me.

BRETT....I can?

SEBASTIAN. That's what I'm here for.

    SEBASTIAN *takes out a business card. Hands it to him*.

    We're in this together, Brett. I told you that on day one.

    BRETT*'s relieved*.

BRETT. That's really… that means a lot, Sebastian. Thank you.

SEBASTIAN. Thank *you*. For your dedication. If only there
    were more like you.

    SEBASTIAN *hands him the card*.

    Keep that safe.

    BRETT *tucks it away in his jacket pocket. He gets up*.

    Just try to stay in the moment. The truth is always in the
    moment. Lay the foundations. The cathedral comes later.

    SEBASTIAN *sits back, smiles*.

    I made that up myself.

Eight

Notre-Dame appears, along with the Eiffel Tower and the Tuileries Garden. Music.

A montage of BRETT *and* CASEY *being lovers in Paris – similar to the montage in Dublin but much faster and at speed – like everything is now on fast-forward.*

CASEY *and* BRETT *pointing with delight at the Eiffel Tower, cycling a bike, eating a baguette.* CASEY *placing a beret on* BRETT'*s head and laughing raucously. Going through all the motions of love, as seen in a Hollywood movie circa the 1940s, and ending with* BRETT *artfully twirling* CASEY *in a Parisian street, then kissing her passionately just like the famous* Kiss by the Hôtel de Ville *in Paris…*

Fade.

Nine

CASEY'*s flat.*

CYNTHIA *and* CASEY *are in the garden, hanging washing on a washing line.*

CASEY *is talking animated, excited.*

CASEY. It was so beautiful, Cynthia, I swear to god I've never seen anywhere like it.

CYNTHIA. Really?

CASEY. I thought I was dead.

CYNTHIA. What?

CASEY. It was that good.

CYNTHIA. Oh.

CASEY. All the jardins and boulevards and boulangeries. And the women are *so* stylish. But then they hardly ever eat.

CYNTHIA. They hardly ever eat like pigs.

CASEY. I wish I could wear a scarf the way French women wear scarves. Just tied at the neck, with nonchalance.

CYNTHIA. It's hard to wear a scarf like that. You need ballerina physique.

CASEY. Brett bought me one to try.

CYNTHIA. Well try. If you want to – try.

CASEY. It's Hermès.

CYNTHIA. Right.

CASEY. Silk. It's the most beautiful thing in the world.

CYNTHIA. Oh for god's sake – would you listen to yourself?

CASEY. What?

CYNTHIA. How could it be the most beautiful thing in the world? It's a scarf.

CASEY. Cynthia.

CYNTHIA. Everything can't be so wonderful and so great and so perfect all the time. This is real life.

CASEY. What's wrong with you?

CYNTHIA *looks at the line. All the clothes on it are men's.*

CYNTHIA. Did you hear about this thing called feminism? Men wash their own clothes.

CASEY *looks at the washing line.*

CASEY. I like doing things for Brett.

CYNTHIA. I'm sure.

CASEY. You don't understand –

CYNTHIA. Actually, Casey, I do understand. Actually I have a lot better grasp on these things than you do. And this stage you're in now, it's called infatuation. And it doesn't last.

CASEY. Maybe not for you.

CYNTHIA. No, for everyone.

CASEY *buries herself in the washing basket.*

There are patterns to these things, okay. First you're looking for common ground. All the similarities between you, like you both like Paris and – *Gone with the Wind*, which I think is a very odd choice of film for a man to have as a favourite but there you are. You might progress beyond that a bit – you might ask about his political beliefs, where he stands on the national question –

CASEY. The same as me.

CYNTHIA. Fine. Of course. But there's going to come a time when you come upon a difference. Something that you can't or don't or won't agree on and it's how you handle those differences, Casey, that's going to be the key. How are you and Brett going to be together and alone in this relationship?

CASEY. We've sorted that out.

CYNTHIA. How?

CASEY. He's only here three days a week.

CYNTHIA. I mean after you're married.

CASEY. So do I.

CYNTHIA. ...Brett's only going to be here three days a week?

CASEY. We think it's best.

CYNTHIA. What?

CASEY. That way we won't get tired of each other, or start taking each other for granted the way a lot of married people seem to. Brett and I want to keep that special spark.

CYNTHIA *stares at her, incredulous*.

CYNTHIA. And where does Brett intend to spend the other four days of his week?

CASEY *shrugs, goes back to the washing*.

CASEY. That's really not my business.

CYNTHIA. You're marrying the man.

CASEY. I trust him.

CYNTHIA. You trust him.

> CASEY *turns her back on* CYNTHIA.

> CYNTHIA *looks at her suspicious.*

…Why are you suddenly working two jobs?

CASEY. What?

CYNTHIA. Sharon Kinsella saw you handing out flyers in town last week.

CASEY. I'm… paying the bills.

CYNTHIA. You paid the bills on one job perfectly well before now. Is Brett working two jobs?

CASEY. Brett works very hard. What about Eric – he's not working?

CYNTHIA. That's totally different, Eric used to be very successful.

CASEY. Look I can't just hop off to Paris at a moment's notice on a marketing assistant's salary.

CYNTHIA. I thought Brett paid for the trip to Paris.

> CASEY *goes back to hanging.*

CASEY. …He – did.

CYNTHIA. Casey –

CASEY. I know what you're trying to do, Cynthia.

CYNTHIA. I'm *trying* to look out for you.

CASEY. I've got Brett doing that.

CYNTHIA. Well I'm not sure he's quite the right person. This whole set-up sounds very convenient for him if you don't mind me saying.

CASEY. You just don't want me to be happy.

CYNTHIA. That's not – of course I want you to be happy, but you're a *depressive*. There are things you need to look out for.

CASEY. I'm looking out for them.

CYNTHIA. You don't even know what they are.

CASEY. And you do?

CYNTHIA. Yes.

CASEY. You know?

CYNTHIA. I've had a little more practice frankly – yes.

CASEY. How?

CYNTHIA. BECAUSE I'M A HAPPILY MARRIED WOMAN AND YOU'RE NOT.

Silence.

Ten

CASEY*'s flat.*

BRETT, ERIC *and* ALAN *are drinking beers in the living room.*

ERIC. We don't do this sort of thing enough, do we? Hang out. The men.

ALAN. Well I thought it'd be good. Have some time to – shoot the breeze, get to know each other, what?

ERIC. The men.

ALAN. Yeah.

They clink bottles. BRETT *seems a little awkward.*

Thanks for having us, Brett.

BRETT. My pleasure.

ALAN. Sorry if we put you on the spot.

BRETT. Not at all. We like – entertaining.

ERIC. Well I was delighted to get out. Been going stir crazy at home truth be told.

ALAN. No luck on the work front, eh, Eric?

ERIC. Well some, some – interest – (*Quickly.*) I'm thinking of joining the gym actually.

ALAN. Oh yeah?

ERIC. Just as something to… You work out, don't you, Brett?

BRETT. A little.

ERIC. Yeah. I… well Cynthia mentioned it actually. That you work out. Which I don't mind – I'm all for self-improvement. Improving the self.

BRETT. It's a continual process.

ERIC. Indeed… indeed.

    ALAN *shakes his head.*

ALAN. You modern men.

ERIC. Not sure it's my thing though – the gym. Seems a bit vain or – no offence, Brett.

ALAN. Don't know until you go.

ERIC. True.

ALAN. And how does anyone know what their – thing is anyway? Take you, Brett. Good-looking man like yourself, you could probably have your choice of women. But you like Casey and that's your thing.

    BRETT *takes an uncomfortable drink.*

BRETT. Yeah.

ALAN. Who are we to judge? Who are we to say what's right or wrong. That's your own business. It's your own choice.

BRETT. Yes.

ALAN. It's between the two of ye.

ERIC. Though we do usually have an idea of what we like and don't like, don't we, Alan?

    ALAN *shrugs.*

ALAN. Not always. You never know – could wake up one morning and give yourself the shock of your life. I know a thing or two about being pushed out of my comfort zone.

ERIC. Really?

ALAN. Oh yes.

ERIC. Because of Barbara?

ALAN. Barbara?

ERIC. Well older man, younger…

ALAN. No, no nothing to do with Barbara! Sunday school. Taught me everything I needed to know in that department. Never judge a book by its… you know.

ERIC. Forgot you were a Protestant, Alan.

ALAN. Oh yes. Prods. Good polished shoes, sensible lunches.

BRETT. And this – pushed you out of your comfort zone?

ALAN. My first day of Sunday school certainly did. Started with my teacher, Ms Snow.

ERIC. Ms – Snow?

BRETT. What an evocative name.

ALAN *nods*.

ALAN. It was my first day, I was new and I was shy and Ms Snow very kindly, took me up to the top of the class and asked where I wanted to sit. And I remember looking round the room… and my gaze fell on this absolutely gorgeous creature with very dark skin. Black hair to just above her shoulders – big, mournful brown eyes.

And she smiled at me. And I can honestly say so help me god, that I had never seen anything more beautiful in my seven-year-old life. Cos this country, in those days… And well, I'll be a bit vulgar here, lads – but I felt a bit of a stirring… and I pointed at the source. My brown-eyed siren. And I said to Ms Snow, 'I'll sit there.'

So I sat down.

And I took out my crayons and I gazed at her and we coloured like this for a while. And all was going well. We were very content. Until Ms Snow walks by and in her innocence, picks up my new girlfriend's picture of a large blue whale and holds it up above her head and in front of the whole class says – 'Look what Khalid has done, everyone. Hasn't he a great old eye for the detail?'

And I realised then that while Khalid may have had a great old eye for the detail, I most certainly did not.

BRETT. You didn't know he was a he.

ALAN. I did not know he was a he, Brett.

Silence.

ALAN *looks at* BRETT *and* ERIC.

BRETT. Gosh.

ERIC. That's quite a story, Alan.

ALAN *suddenly feels self-conscious.*

ALAN. Yeah. (*Then.*) Don't know why I told it now.

ALAN *takes a tense sip of beer.*

CYNTHIA *marches in.*

CYNTHIA. Eric, we're going!

ERIC. What?

CYNTHIA. Casey's asked us to leave.

ALAN. What do you mean she's asked ye to leave?

CASEY *follows her.*

CASEY. I didn't say anything about Eric.

CYNTHIA. No fine. Just me.

CYNTHIA *moves to grab her things.*

BRETT. Hang on – what's happening?

CASEY. Stay out of it, Brett.

CYNTHIA. Are you coming, Eric?

ERIC. I haven't finished my beer.

CYNTHIA. Is that low-fat?

ERIC. I don't – know. /

ALAN. I don't understand – are you two fighting?

CYNTHIA. No. /

CASEY. Yes.

ALAN. About what?

CYNTHIA. Forget it. Eric, do you want to stay?

ERIC. Well we were just in the middle of a very interesting –

CYNTHIA. Okay fine –

ALAN. Girls, please. What is happening?

CASEY. This is my flat. There are certain things I don't have to listen to.

BRETT. Casey –

CASEY. Leave it, Brett.

CYNTHIA (*to* ERIC). Just give me the keys.

ERIC. Do you want me to come with you?

CYNTHIA. I don't care.

CASEY. I'm going to my room.

ALAN. Casey, be reasonable.

CYNTHIA. There's no point. She's not in her right mind.

CASEY *turns* –

CASEY. Yes I am! Don't you say that! This is just like the *Home and Away* theme tune all over again.

CYNTHIA. Oh for Christ's sake. /

CASEY. Remember that, Dad?

ALAN. What? /

CASEY. The *Home and Away* theme tune.

ALAN. I don't know what you're /

CYNTHIA. It was over twenty years ago.

CASEY. They were having a talent day in school and everyone had to pick a party piece and whoever sang the best song got a prize and I had the idea to pick the *Home and Away* theme tune –

CYNTHIA. No you didn't /

CASEY. Cos no one else was going to sing that, but Cynthia kept telling me it was stupid and everyone would laugh –

CYNTHIA. Cos you were off-key /

CASEY. So I lost my nerve and changed my mind and sang that song from *The Little Mermaid* that *everyone* sang –

CYNTHIA. I was saving you from yourself –

CASEY. And then Cynthia sang the theme tune from *Home and Away* –

ERIC *gasps*.

ERIC. You didn't!

CASEY. *And* won the prize herself.

ERIC. No.

Everyone looks at CYNTHIA.

CYNTHIA. That is not how I remember it.

ALAN. I don't remember it at all.

CASEY. There was nothing wrong with how I sang the song.

CYNTHIA. Well.

CASEY *turns to* BRETT, *utterly earnest and starts to sing the* Home and Away *theme tune*.

CYNTHIA *cuts in over her*.

No it's –

CYNTHIA *starts singing the* Home and Away *theme tune over* CASEY.

CASEY *starts singing the* Home and Away *theme tune even louder over* CYNTHIA.

CYNTHIA *starts singing even louder over* CASEY.

They keep singing, louder and louder until –

ALAN. GIRLS, PLEASE!

CASEY. Which of us sings it better?

ALAN. You're both – very strong.

CASEY. Brett?

> BRETT *is at a loss.*

BRETT. …The past shouldn't dictate the present, Casey.

> CASEY *looks at him, upset.*

ERIC. Wow.

CYNTHIA. This is pathetic. I'm going. Eric?

ERIC. Okay.

> ERIC *gets up and follows* CYNTHIA *to the door. He waves to the men, awkward –*

> We should do this again some time.

> *He and* CYNTHIA *head out.* CASEY *shouts after her –*

CASEY. You stole my song, Cynthia!

> CYNTHIA *slams the door.*

> *Silence.*

> *No one quite knows what to do.*

> BRETT *nervously moves towards* CASEY, *trying to console her.*

BRETT. Hey.

> CASEY *screams in frustration –*

CASEY. I hate her!

> *She runs out or upstairs.*

BRETT. Casey!

> BRETT *and* ALAN *are left alone.*

ALAN. …Well. That was fun.

BRETT. Should I… go after her?

ALAN. Nah, leave her be. You know what sisters are like.

> BRETT *looks after her, concerned.*

BRETT. Yes.

> ALAN *looks up, interested.*

ALAN. You have some yourself?

BRETT. No. But... I can imagine.

ALAN. Brothers?

BRETT. I'm an only child.

ALAN. Ah. We don't know much about your background, do we, Brett?

BRETT *glances back towards the door, still wondering if he should follow her.*

We've been getting these crank phone calls at home, you know.

BRETT *turns, surprised.*

BRETT....Crank phone calls?

ALAN. Some weirdo breathing down the receiver late at night.

BRETT. God.

ALAN. Yeah.

BRETT. Who do you think it is?

ALAN. Dunno... not you, is it?

BRETT. Me?

ALAN. I'm joking.

BRETT. I would never –

ALAN. I know, Brett. It was a joke. Relax.

BRETT *is now deeply uncomfortable. He reaches into his pocket and pulls out the card* SEBASTIAN *gave him.*

He turns it in his hands, fidgeting, anxious.

ALAN *studies him, trying to phrase this the right way.*

Listen, Brett, the thing is... you and Casey... it just seems a bit –

Suddenly –

BRETT. I'm sorry, Mr Cassidy, I forgot. I've to do – something.

ALAN. Do something?

BRETT. A phone call. (*Quickly.*) Not that kind of phone call. It's urgent.

ALAN.…Oh.

BRETT. I'll be back in a – minute. Sorry.

BRETT *rushes off with the card and his phone*.

ALAN *sits back and takes an unsettled sip of beer*.

ALAN.…Did I overshare?

Eleven

CASEY *is back in* TESS*'s office, covering her face with her hands*.

There is the distinct air of frustration from TESS.

TESS. I'm sure it wasn't that bad.

CASEY. She did it on purpose! She wants to drive him away.

TESS. Well that's not going to happen.

CASEY. Isn't it?

TESS.…Is it?

TESS *consults her notes*.

CASEY *looks up*.

CASEY. Well I don't *want* it to happen, obviously.

TESS. No.

TESS *puts down the notes*.

CASEY. But I just don't trust that it won't. Because I'm me. And this is how it's always been for me. This is how it goes.

TESS *takes a slightly frustrated breath*.

TESS. I thought we weren't going to talk like that any more.

CASEY *looks a bit sheepish.*

I thought we were here to change the story.

CASEY. I know and we are, it's just… well I'm not sure I really believe the story *can* be changed. For me.

TESS *sighs, frustrated.*

TESS. Okay. I'm afraid we're out of time.

CASEY. But we've only just –

TESS. There's something we should discuss.

TESS *looks at her.*

Your card this month was declined.

CASEY.…Oh.

TESS. Are you having some money –

CASEY. No.

TESS. Because if you are, we need to talk about that.

CASEY. I'm not.

TESS *looks at her.*

TESS. You're about to undertake a very serious financial obligation, Casey, if you're not able –

CASEY (*quickly*). I am able.

TESS. But if you need to take a break, now is the –

CASEY. I don't want to take a break.

TESS. Casey –

CASEY (*suddenly*). We took a trip to Paris that's all!

TESS *stops.*

TESS. Paris?

TESS *consults her notes.*

That's not in my notes.

CASEY *seems slightly worried.*

CASEY. It was – Brett's suggestion.

TESS *looks up, annoyed*.

TESS. What do you mean it was Brett's suggestion?

CASEY (*quickly*). I didn't mind. I was happy. And I thought –

TESS (*voice rising*). It doesn't matter what you think, Casey.
You don't make these decisions on your own.

CASEY *shrinks back*.

CASEY. I'll pay next week.

TESS. Next week you'll be two weeks late.

CASEY. I'll get the money, I promise.

TESS. People take advantage of new businesses, Casey. We
can't just –

CASEY (*desperate*). I don't want a break. Please. I'll get the
money.

CASEY *looks at her, desperate*.

Please.

Then TESS *seems to concede*.

TESS. …I'll have to run it by upstairs.

CASEY *breathes, visibly relieved*.

But next time… there'll be no next time.

Twelve

CYNTHIA *stands in* BRETT *and* CASEY*'s doorway.*

BRETT. I'm not supposed to let you in. I'm under strict instructions.

CYNTHIA *holds out a box of chocolates.*

CYNTHIA. What if I come bearing gifts?

BRETT. Casey said, two words. 'Trojan Horse.'

CYNTHIA. Right.

BRETT.…She's not here though. She's out. I'm making dinner. Do you want to – leave a note or something?

She regards him warily.

CYNTHIA.…Okay.

CYNTHIA *steps inside.*

I thought you were only here three days a week.

BRETT. Today is one of them.

CYNTHIA. But Casey's working?

BRETT. It's how the schedule worked out. Tea?

CYNTHIA. No. Schedule?

BRETT. Work's been busy. Water?

CYNTHIA. Yes please. So the landscape gardening's… going well?

BRETT. Yeah great. I've all these clients outside the city so the days I'm not with Casey I'm… on the road.

BRETT *goes to get the water.*

CYNTHIA. And now you're just here – making dinner?

BRETT. She likes me to be here even when she's not.

CYNTHIA *looks around the place, almost suspiciously.*

So, how did you get into television? Did you take a course?

CYNTHIA. A course? No. I didn't take a course.

BRETT. You had some contacts?

CYNTHIA. No I had no contacts whatsoever.

BRETT. You must have done something right.

CYNTHIA. Not really.

He hands her the glass.

BRETT. You don't want to talk about it. Okay. That's fine…
I'm just going to start the food.

He puts on an apron.

She watches.

CYNTHIA.… You like cooking huh?

BRETT. Sure.

CYNTHIA. What do you like about it?

BRETT. The creativity. Sometimes I pretend I'm on one of
those shows.

CYNTHIA. You look like you could be on one of those shows.

He hands her a piece of chopped veg.

She eats it.

Eric never cooks dinner. He can eat. God, he can eat. But he
doesn't cook.

BRETT. Well, I'm sure he has other strengths.

CYNTHIA. Me too.

BRETT *begins to chop. She watches.*

…I got lucky.

BRETT *looks at her.*

BRETT. Sorry?

CYNTHIA. That's how I got into television… I got lucky. I was
walking through a supermarket one day and I saw this guy
looking at me and he kept looking and looking and eventually
he came over and said that he thought I had a good face for
television. He asked if I'd ever done any. And I said no and he
gave me his card and he said come in for a screen test. And
I went in for a screen test. And he gave me some stuff to read
and I read it on camera and he said he wanted to give me

a job. He said start Monday. So I started Monday. And that's how I got into television.

BRETT. Oh.

CYNTHIA. It's also how I met Eric.

BRETT. Through the job?

CYNTHIA. No, that was him. The guy in the supermarket. That was Eric.

BRETT. Oh.

CYNTHIA. He gave me the job so he could get in my pants.

BRETT. And your mom thinks that's a nice story?

CYNTHIA. He tells it slightly differently. Puts the emphasis on winning me over. It's basically a romcom – we get married in the end.

She laughs, hollow.

He was let go from the station last year. They had to make some cuts. They kept me on.

BRETT. That must be hard.

CYNTHIA. On him or me?

BRETT. On both of you.

She eats another vegetable, watching him.

I really do like the show. There are times it's really made me think.

CYNTHIA. Eric thinks it's trite. Which rhymes with shite. Which he thinks most things are. He's hard to please since he was made redundant.

BRETT. I'm sure he'll feel better when he starts this documentary.

CYNTHIA. No one's going to make that documentary.

BRETT. But he said –

CYNTHIA. Eric hasn't thought of a good idea in years. His producing days are over. I'm just waiting for it to sink in.

Beat.

Don't tell anyone I said that.

BRETT. Okay.

CYNTHIA. Do you pride yourself on being a good listener?
I seem to be talking a lot.

BRETT. …I just find it easy I guess.

CYNTHIA. What?

BRETT. Talking to you.

He hands her another vegetable. They look at one another.

A vibe.

It frightens CYNTHIA. *She decides to say something dangerous.*

CYNTHIA. Casey's a manic-depressive, you know.

BRETT. Excuse me?

CYNTHIA. Bipolar disorder they call it now.

BRETT. Oh yeah, I know.

CYNTHIA. You know?

BRETT. Yes.

CYNTHIA. She's told you?

BRETT. Yes.

CYNTHIA. And you're okay with that?

BRETT. Of course.

She stares at him, wanting to provoke something.

CYNTHIA. She's been hospitalised, you know.

BRETT. A long time ago.

CYNTHIA. When she was seventeen. She was so depressed she
couldn't even get up to go to the toilet. She started wetting
the bed.

BRETT. She's told me all about it.

CYNTHIA. She told you she wet the bed?

BRETT. Yes.

CYNTHIA. Jesus.

BRETT. What?

CYNTHIA. I just thought the point of new relationships was to
keep the shameful stuff to yourself so you could still be
found attractive.

BRETT. I presume she wanted to be honest… and I do still find
her attractive.

He starts cutting again.

CYNTHIA *watches.*

CYNTHIA.…Let's be honest here, Brett. I don't trust you.

He stops and looks at her, a bit startled.

I mean you're doing a great job of the whole, sensitive
new-age-man thing, but you don't know what you're dealing
with, with Casey.

BRETT. Casey's told me everything.

CYNTHIA. Really?

BRETT. Yes. She told me she felt desolate and she didn't know
why. She told me that some days she couldn't get out of bed
and on others she'd be moving so fast she could outrun
speeding buses. She told me that she spent a thousand euros in
Mothercare on items for babies that didn't exist. She told me
that they had to medicate her and the medication was so strong
that for three whole weeks in hospital she didn't have enough
energy to mouth her own name. She told me it was terrifying.
She told me that she wanted to die. She's told me all that.
I know all that. So you won't get anywhere pulling skeletons
out of Casey's closet. She's already told me the worst.

Silence.

CYNTHIA *seems shocked by his sudden passion.*

CYNTHIA.…We worry about her.

BRETT. Well if you don't mind me saying I think it's
patronising.

CYNTHIA. Why are you going out with her?

BRETT. Why would you ask a thing like that?

CYNTHIA. Because no one else would touch her with a ten-foot pole.

Beat.

I'm sorry – that was insensitive… I'll rephrase. She's got problems.

BRETT. Who doesn't?

CYNTHIA. Why are you in such a rush to marry her? Is this what you do – prey on sad, unhappy women?

BRETT. I don't think Casey's the one who's unhappy.

CYNTHIA. Excuse me?

BRETT. She seems pretty on top of her choices. You, I'm not so sure of.

CYNTHIA. What?

BRETT. Wasn't that the point of your story?

CYNTHIA. What story?

BRETT. The story of how you met your husband. You were there in the supermarket and the guy spots you and tells you you're beautiful and he thinks you might have talent. And you think – this is it. I'm all set. I'm gonna be a big TV star and marry a hotshot producer, and everything's gonna be hunky-dory. Except he's not a hotshot producer he's just some klutz they're going to fire –

CYNTHIA. Don't talk about Eric like that.

BRETT. – and you're not a big success – you're presenting a mediocre weather show.

CYNTHIA. You said it made you think.

BRETT. You're stuck, Cynthia.

CYNTHIA. How dare you!

BRETT. Mired in disappointment. Choking on unfulfilled dreams. Your marriage contract nothing but a noose around your neck pulling tighter and tighter with each passing year.

CYNTHIA *stares at him, like he's seen into her soul.*

You're trapped... Aren't you, Cynthia?

Very slowly, she nods.

You thought it was going to be so much more than this, didn't you? You thought it was going to be so much better?

She nods again, suddenly close to tears.

CYNTHIA. Yes... I did. I – did. I thought our marriage would be an adventure. I thought he was going straight to the top and I was going with him. I thought we were going to have one of those lives you read about in weekend supplements – a power couple.

BRETT. But instead –

CYNTHIA. Instead he's on the sofa, eating crisps and watching *Coronation Street*, losing his ambition and his muscle tone in one undignified swoop. And the weather in this country is always the same. This isn't what I signed up for.

She looks at him.

BRETT. No.

CYNTHIA. It's crushing me.

BRETT. I know.

CYNTHIA. How do you know?... How come you're so easy to talk to?

BRETT. I was just thinking the same about you!

CYNTHIA. Really?

BRETT. It's like I don't even have to think. It just flows.

BRETT looks at her, suddenly excited.

I was completely in the moment there. I mean that had an effect on you, didn't it – what I just said about you being trapped?

CYNTHIA. Yes.

BRETT. You were moved?

CYNTHIA. I was.

BRETT smiles, exhilarated.

BRETT. You don't know how good that makes me feel.

He laughs. She laughs.

Wow.

CYNTHIA. Wow.

BRETT. Wow.

CYNTHIA. Wow.

They look at one another. A moment.

And suddenly they fall into a passionate embrace.

It goes on for some time before BRETT *breaks away.*

BRETT. Oh my god.

CYNTHIA. Oh my god.

BRETT. I can't believe we just –

CYNTHIA. That was fucking incredible.

She looks at him.

Do it again.

She lunges towards him.

BRETT. No!

CYNTHIA. Please.

BRETT. No, Jesus. This can't happen.

CYNTHIA. Of course it can.

He pushes her away.

BRETT. I've done too much work.

CYNTHIA. Work?… Like therapy? God you're so emotionally available.

He tries to get things back on track.

BRETT. I – love Casey.

CYNTHIA. Oh don't be so fucking moralistic – two seconds ago you couldn't keep your hands off me.

He shakes his head, desperate, beginning to crumble.

BRETT. I didn't mean it.

CYNTHIA. You didn't mean it? Come on.

BRETT. You have to leave right now.

CYNTHIA. Look, Brett –

He tries to usher her out desperately.

BRETT. Please, please. Please.

CYNTHIA. Brett /

BRETT. Go go go /

CYNTHIA. You're being hysterical!

She slaps him.

God, this is so sexy.

She kisses him again. He breaks away.

BRETT. Cynthia, you've no idea what I've just done.

CYNTHIA. I did it too, we couldn't help ourselves.

BRETT. But I've broken the contract. /

CYNTHIA. Yes but... what contract?

BRETT. I could be out of work for years.

CYNTHIA. What are you talking about? You're – on a contract?

She recoils.

...*Are* you a prostitute?

BRETT *reaches into his pocket and pulls out the card to call* SEBASTIAN.

BRETT. I have to get me head straight.

CYNTHIA. Wait...

He takes out his phone, panicked.

BRETT. I need to make a call.

CYNTHIA.... What's happened to your voice?

He tries to dial but he's jittery.

BRETT. You can't stay here.

CYNTHIA. Why are you suddenly talking like that?

BRETT. Cynthia, for fuck's sake.

CYNTHIA. Are you from… *Donaghmede*?

> *He stares at her, helpless.*

> What the hell is going on here, Brett?

> *Suddenly she snatches* SEBASTIAN*'s card out of his hand.*

BRETT. Hey. Give that back.

> CYNTHIA *stares at the card then up at him.*

CYNTHIA. What is this?

> *He reaches for it. She holds it away.*

BRETT. Give it to me, Cynthia, I'm not joking.

> *Suddenly he grabs her, violent.*

> Give it fucking back.

CYNTHIA (*shocked, frightened*). Brett…

> *A beat.*

> *Then he lets her go.*

BRETT. Oh Jesus.

> *He steps back, shocked at himself.*

> Oh Jesus Jesus Jesus – oh no.

> *Suddenly he turns and runs out of the house.*

> CYNTHIA *calls after him.*

CYNTHIA. Brett! Where are you – Brett!

> *She looks at the card.*

> (*Calling.*) Is that even your name?

In another time and place across the city, we see CASEY, *pale and tired and wearing a T-shirt with a company logo, as she approaches various people – or audience members – with flyers.*

CASEY (*to the passers-by*). Hello sorry could I have a moment of your –

People ignore her or don't answer. She tries again.

Hey there sorry could I have a moment of your – time? Are you happy with your current internet provider?

People walk on. She keeps handing out leaflets.

Hi there sorry could I've a moment of your – are you happy with your current –

She stops.

Are you...

She stops, she looks at us.

Black.

ACT TWO

One

A spotlight on a stage.

SEBASTIAN *walks into it, holding a sword.*

He looks at us. Intense. Beat.

SEBASTIAN.
Friends. Romans. Countrymen. Lend me your ears;
I come to bury Caesar, not to praise him.

He stops. Shakes it off.

I was never a convincing Mark Antony.

Not my part. Too obvious.

TESS. Okay.

TESS *appears with a clipboard and tries to take the sword.*

SEBASTIAN. I'll hang on to it, helps me think.

TESS *looks up and indicates for them to bring up the lights.*

The spotlight disappears. The auditorium lights come up.

And a group of people are standing onstage behind
SEBASTIAN. *They are all holding scripts, and dressed*
in black.

SEBASTIAN *turns to them. They look at him, eager.*

Right. So this is the theatre.

ACTOR 1. Oh /

ACTOR 2. Lovely /

ACTOR 3. Gorgeous space. /

SEBASTIAN. Where the magic happens. Occasionally.

ACTOR 1. And is this where we'll be –

SEBASTIAN. Well.

ACTOR 1 (*quickly*). If we get picked.

SEBASTIAN. For role-play exercises, improvisations, assessments it helps to be *in the space*.

They nod, earnest.

But the rest of the time, we'll be out in the field.

ACTORS. Right. / Yeah. / Course.

SEBASTIAN. In the theatre of life.

He laughs.

They laugh, dutifully.

TESS *starts handing out sheets to the group.*

TESS. You'll each need to sign one of these before we start.

SEBASTIAN *makes his way over to a desk at the far side of the stage.*

There are piles of scripts on it and two chairs.

ACTOR 3 (*re: the contract*). Is this – legally binding?

SEBASTIAN. One hundred per cent.

ACTOR 3. I just wonder… if I should have someone check it?

TESS. Then you'll have to come back another time.

SEBASTIAN. We can't see you otherwise.

ACTOR 3 *looks around.*

The rest of them are signing so he/she does.

ACTOR 3.…I'm sure it's fine.

SEBASTIAN. Shall we begin?

TESS. Hang on – there's an order.

SEBASTIAN (*mocking her*). Oooh an order. She loves an order.

TESS (*ignoring*). We'll start with number one-one-five.

SEBASTIAN. Why are we starting with one-one-five?

TESS. Because that's what the PA has written down.

SEBASTIAN. Why?

TESS. God knows. (*Annoyed*.) I'm not the PA, Sebastian. (*Calling*.) One-one-five? Anyone here got one-one-five?

The ACTORS *look around.*

ACTORS. No. / Nope. / Sorry.

TESS. Shit.

TESS starts rifling through some sheets, stressed.

SEBASTIAN rolls his eyes.

SEBASTIAN. Worse than the RSC.

ACTOR 1 steps forward.

ACTOR 2. Sorry, but we won't be going beyond four, will we? It's just I have a thing.

SEBASTIAN. Creativity cannot be coerced.

TESS shakes her head behind him and mouths 'no'.

We're looking for commitment. In everything you do.

ACTOR 2 (*re:* TESS). Okay, cool.

TESS (*stressed*). Alright if you could all wait backstage until your number's called, I'll call the PA and try to sort this –

Suddenly CYNTHIA *enters through a side door. She's holding* SEBASTIAN*'s card and looking round –*

CYNTHIA. Oh sorry.

Everyone looks over.

I'm looking for –

TESS. Are you one-one-five?

CYNTHIA. Excuse me?

TESS. Are you number – one-one-five?

CYNTHIA. …Eh. Yes. But –

TESS (*relieved*). Fantastic. Take a seat.

The rest of the ACTORS *move off, eyeing* CYNTHIA *resentfully.*

As she makes her way onto the stage, SEBASTIAN *looks up at the lighting box. Signals.*

SEBASTIAN. Thanks. Let's reinstate the –

The lights change.

And now we are in the office where we first saw BRETT *meet* SEBASTIAN.

SEBASTIAN *gestures to a chair.* CYNTHIA *hesitantly sits.*

CYNTHIA....Sorry but am I in the right –

SEBASTIAN *gestures for her to stop talking.*

He picks up a pen and starts filling in a form.

SEBASTIAN. First things first. Name.

CYNTHIA. Cynthia Cassidy.

He writes.

SEBASTIAN. ID?

CYNTHIA. Oh... em...

CYNTHIA *roots through her purse.*

...only a driver's licence.

SEBASTIAN *hands the licence to* TESS.

SEBASTIAN. Agent?

CYNTHIA....Do I need one?

SEBASTIAN *and* TESS *glances at one another.*

TESS. Not necessarily.

SEBASTIAN. They only take another ten per cent. Age range?

CYNTHIA. Age range?

SEBASTIAN. What's your playing age range?

CYNTHIA. Are you asking me my age?

SEBASTIAN. Women always lie.

TESS. Well of course women lie – from twenty-five on they're playing Jack Nicholson's mother – am I right? Why wouldn't they fecking lie?

SEBASTIAN. Alright it's a cruel business we all know that.

He studies CYNTHIA.

I'll put eighteen to – seventy.

He writes it down.

And no criminal record?

CYNTHIA. Criminal –

SEBASTIAN. We can still work with it but we need the facts.

CYNTHIA....no.

TESS. Great.

CYNTHIA. I'm sorry is this –

TESS. And you've signed the NDA?

CYNTHIA. NDA?

SEBASTIAN. Oh you have to sign the NDA. Nothing in this room can be repeated outside it.

TESS. Obviously.

SEBASTIAN. We can sue.

CYNTHIA. But I just –

TESS. We can't go any further until you've signed.

TESS hands her the page.

CYNTHIA *quickly signs the NDA. She hands it back.*

SEBASTIAN. Excellent. Right. Whenever you like.

CYNTHIA *looks at them, confused.*

A beat.

CYNTHIA....Sorry?

SEBASTIAN. The floor is yours.

SEBASTIAN points to a spot onstage. A spotlight appears.

CYNTHIA (*confused*). Oh no... I think there's been a –

SEBASTIAN. It just gives us a flavour. Anything will do – your Hedda, your Ophelia, your Helen of Troy...

CYNTHIA. Helen of Troy?

TESS. Someone once did *Mrs Brown's Boys*.

SEBASTIAN. Don't, Tess, please.

TESS. I'm taking the pressure off.

CYNTHIA. I don't understand –

TESS. What about a poem?

SEBASTIAN *slams down his pen, annoyed.*

SEBASTIAN. Why do people always assume poets and playwrights are the same thing?

TESS. I'm just /

SEBASTIAN. It's an entirely different art form! One is essentially dramatic, the other –

TESS (*irritated*). Sebastian, we just need to see what she's got.

He sighs.

CYNTHIA *shifts nervously, unsure what to do.*

CYNTHIA. I – did do a poem once… in a feis.

SEBASTIAN (*annoyed*). Fine. Do a poem.

TESS. Great.

CYNTHIA *gets up and walks tentatively to the spotlight. She steps in.*

CYNTHIA.…Like this?

TESS *nods encouragingly.*

TESS. Uh-huh.

SEBASTIAN (*to* TESS *under his breath*). Why do they never come prepared?

CYNTHIA *smooths her hair, warming to the idea of performing.*

CYNTHIA. Okay… let's see. Oh! What about a song?

SEBASTIAN *looks like he might cry.*

SEBASTIAN. A song? Now look, there's a place for musical theatre but I have no idea where it is.

TESS (*quickly*). Sure that's fine, give us a song.

A few sniggers from the ACTORS *behind alerts* CYNTHIA *to the fact this might have been a mistake.*

She glances round feeling nervous.

CYNTHIA....okay.

A beat. She takes a breath.

Then she steps forward and earnestly and exquisitely, like she is singing the most beautiful aria, heartbreaking and profound, she begins to sing the Home and Away *theme tune.*

SEBASTIAN *lifts his head, surprised.*

TESS *looks up.*

CYNTHIA *keeps going, tentative but growing more assured.*

As she continues to sing, the ACTORS *behind start to subtly harmonise.*

CYNTHIA *keeps singing, her confidence growing – perhaps* TESS *starts to sway very subtly getting into it.*

CYNTHIA, *now lost in the song, takes a breath, ready for the big finish, when –*

SEBASTIAN. Thank you! Next part's a stretch, I'm not sure you have the range but – good. Brave choice.

TESS *takes out a tissue, wipes her eyes.*

(*Re:* TESS.) ...What's happening here?

TESS *is embarrassed.*

TESS. I was moved.

SEBASTIAN*'s surprised.*

SEBASTIAN. By that?

TESS. It's very on-brand for our clientele.

SEBASTIAN *rolls his eyes.*

Look there's no point them doing a great Antigone if they can't do Susie from Sandymount.

SEBASTIAN. Oh she'd be a very good Susie.

They both look at CYNTHIA.

TESS. Wouldn't she? I was just thinking – with her look and the hair –

SEBASTIAN (*to* CYNTHIA). Can you rollerblade?

CYNTHIA. Rollerblade?… Look I don't know exactly what's – but on the phone she said –

TESS. Oh god, the new PA is a nightmare. She probably didn't explain.

CYNTHIA. Not really. Cos I'm actually looking for –

TESS. Obviously the kinds of scripts you'll be working with here are –

SEBASTIAN. Different.

TESS. Well they're not exactly.

SEBASTIAN. *Medea*.

TESS. No.

SEBASTIAN. Cos matricide's illegal. For now.

TESS. Though we do try and keep them interesting.

SEBASTIAN. Tess is in charge of story –

TESS. In close consultation with the client.

SEBASTIAN. I'm the talent. *With* the talent.

He laughs.

CYNTHIA *frowns, trying to follow.*

TESS. I won't lie, the storylines are somewhat – limited.

SEBASTIAN. Thanks to Hollywood.

TESS. But we try to keep it creative. You can make up your own backstory. Or a new walk or – accent.

CYNTHIA *thinks.*

CYNTHIA. Accent?… Yes, he has an accent.

SEBASTIAN. Who?

TESS. But the client *must* have final approval – that part of the contract is non-negotiable.

CYNTHIA. Contract… he mentioned that too. What is this –

TESS. Think of it like a soap.

SEBASTIAN. You could be in one of those for ten years.

TESS. Longer.

SEBASTIAN. Longer. In the end you might know your character better than anyone.

TESS. You might *think* you know your character better than anyone – and this is the crucial point – though you might *feel* you should have a say over what could or should happen to them – you don't.

SEBASTIAN. But you can make an offer –

TESS. You can't.

SEBASTIAN. Did we finalise that?

TESS. Absolutely.

SEBASTIAN. It just feels a little –

TESS. There has to be a structure, Sebastian. Rules.

SEBASTIAN (*to the others*). She loves a rule.

TESS. The final decision lies with the writer.

SEBASTIAN. I know some don't agree with the privileging of text.

TESS. But here, the writer is –

SEBASTIAN. God.

TESS. Well. The client. The client is god. And the writer is the client, guided by the dramaturg – sometimes quite heavily – which is: me.

TESS *smiles, proud of this*.

SEBASTIAN. 'We are all the authors of our own love story.'
That's our tagline. We'd have put it on the website but –

TESS. We don't have one.

SEBASTIAN. For obvious reasons.

CYNTHIA*'s putting it together.*

CYNTHIA. Oh my god. So… Casey has written this – story?

SEBASTIAN. Casey? You mean O'Casey? Yes he wrote all his –
would you call them stories?

TESS. This is nothing like that.

SEBASTIAN. Though I played Joxer once – to excellent
reviews.

TESS. This is not a play. We've a dedicated ensemble.

SEBASTIAN. On a variety of contracts –

TESS. Short term, long-term –

SEBASTIAN. Lifers. Depending on ability.

TESS. And availability. (*To* CYNTHIA.) What's yours by the
way?

TESS *takes out a pen, ready to write this down.*

CYNTHIA. What's a lifer?

SEBASTIAN. Ah…

TESS (*irritated*). Well we'll get to that. Are you free weekends?

SEBASTIAN. Lifers are our most exclusive package.

TESS *tries to stop him.*

TESS. If you get a callback we'll explain in full –

But SEBASTIAN *is off –*

SEBASTIAN (*over her*). Forget your Brandos, forget your
Streeps, forget your Daniel DLs – these are the real method
actors, the true greats.

TESS. Sebastian, we haven't time. (*To* CYNTHIA.) They're his
special project.

TESS *leans in and whispers to* SEBASTIAN –

I don't think she's a lifer.

SEBASTIAN *looks at* CYNTHIA *and laughs.*

SEBASTIAN. Her? Oh god no.

CYNTHIA. Why aren't I a lifer?

TESS. Lifers are our most dedicated members of the ensemble.

SEBASTIAN. Willing to make the ultimate sacrifice for the sake of their art.

TESS. You're probably looking for something more – part-time?

CYNTHIA. The ultimate sacrifice… (*Realising.*) You mean… *marriage*?

TESS. Let's just see if you get a callback.

CYNTHIA *gasps.*

CYNTHIA. Is Brett a lifer?

TESS. Who's Brett?

CYNTHIA. Brett Bradley. I think he might be one of your – ensemble.

SEBASTIAN. Oh we cannot discuss our ensemble with a potential trainee.

CYNTHIA. But he's got the accent and the weird backstory – is *that* why he's marrying her?

TESS. Are you talking about one of our clients?

SEBASTIAN. We cannot talk about our clients – it's strictly confidential.

CYNTHIA. But is that why he's broken the contract?

SEBASTIAN. We do sign legal clauses too, you know.

CYNTHIA. Cos he wasn't supposed to kiss me?

TESS. What exactly are you talking about?

Suddenly a side door opens in the auditorium and a woman – ACTOR 4 – *rushes in breathless, limping.*

ACTOR 4. I'm so sorry I'm late. You haven't started, have yis?

SEBASTIAN. Who are you?

She holds up a sheet of paper.

ACTOR 4. One-one-five. There were roadworks in town – I did something to me shoe.

SEBASTIAN *looks at* CYNTHIA.

SEBASTIAN. So who are you?

CYNTHIA. I can explain, I just need to –

ACTOR 4 *looks at* CYNTHIA.

ACTOR 4. She's that girl – off the telly.

SEBASTIAN *stares at* CYNTHIA.

SEBASTIAN. What girl?

ACTOR 4. Does that weather show – it's kinda crappy, but some people like it.

CYNTHIA. A lot of people like it.

ACTOR 4. Isn't that against the rules?

SEBASTIAN. Tess, call security.

TESS *picks up the phone.* CYNTHIA *tries to stop him.*

CYNTHIA. No please –

ACTOR 4. Cos like couldn't people recognise her if she's on TV?

CYNTHIA. Look I just found your card and wanted to ask some questions –

SEBASTIAN *snatches the card off her.*

SEBASTIAN. Please leave.

CYNTHIA. I just need to know about these contracts –

SEBASTIAN (*to* TESS). I've changed my mind she's not right for Susie.

CYNTHIA. I think one of your ensemble has a crush on me.

TESS. Please go.

CYNTHIA. He kissed me!

SEBASTIAN. Rejection is part of the actor's life. You must learn to handle it with grace.

CYNTHIA. You don't understand –

He pats her hand.

SEBASTIAN. Ms Cassidy. You're just not what we're looking for.

CYNTHIA *looks at him.*

Maybe she grabs one of the contracts off the desk – before she rushes out.

Lights down.

Two

CASEY*'s living room.*

CASEY *stands, in a pretty dress, nervously holding a piece of paper.*

PAULINE *and* ALAN *sit attentive nearby, listening.*

She's clears her throat self-consciously.

CASEY. 'For Brett. On our wedding day.'

PAULINE *nods, encouraging.*

PAULINE. Very good.

CASEY (*reciting*).
    I know what it is to be poor
    I know what it is to be old
    I know what it is to be deaf and dumb
    I know what it is to be blind

    ALAN *frowns.*

    I know what it is to have doors close on you
    Windows slam in your face
    I know what it is to feel empty
    Just a body and a name

But then I met you
And everything changed…
Now I know what it is to be loved.

She looks up, waiting.

Silence.

ALAN.…Wow.

PAULINE. Hmmn.

Beat.

ALAN. Is it a bit intense though? For a wedding.

CASEY *looks at them.*

CASEY. It's meant to be intense. It's meant to convey how I feel.

ALAN. But what's all that about you being blind and deaf? You were never blind and deaf.

CASEY. It's a metaphor.

PAULINE. Exactly, Alan.

CASEY. For how I felt before I met him.

ALAN. And people'll get that, will they?

CASEY. Well –

ALAN. I think there could be a few more rhymes. People love a rhyme. Blind and kind's a good one.

CASEY *deflates.*

PAULINE. Alan.

ALAN. Or what about that one we had at our wedding?

PAULINE *gasps puts her hand over her heart, emotional at the memory.*

PAULINE. Sonnet 116.

(*Quoting.*)
'Let me not to the marriage of true minds,
Admit impediments.'

ALAN. Gorgeous.

CASEY *is affronted.*

CASEY. Everyone reads that at their wedding.

PAULINE. Not everyone.

CASEY. It's famous.

ALAN. That's good.

CASEY (*annoyed*). I don't want something famous – I want something original. Something no one's ever heard before.

ALAN. I think it's better if it's something people know.

CASEY. Why?

ALAN. Cos then they know it's good.

> CASEY *deflates*.

PAULINE. Alan… (*Trying to reassure*.) Don't mind your father, Casey. I think it's – great you're writing poetry now.

CASEY. You do?

PAULINE. Yes. It's very creative. Brett must be rubbing off on you.

> CASEY *looks up, surprised*.

CASEY. Well I've always written, I just – never –

> She stops. Then changes tack.

> Yes I think he is.

PAULINE. Isn't that wonderful? We always thought Cynthia was the artistic one, didn't we, Alan? But look at you now, a writer, a wedding…

> CASEY *smiles, shyly*.

CASEY. Brett makes me feel like I can do anything. Like I'm a flower in bloom.

ALAN. Now that's poetic. Write that down.

> CASEY *quickly writes this down*.

PAULINE. You know, I had my reservations about Brett early on. Only natural. What with my own disappointments.

> She looks pointedly at ALAN, who rolls his eyes.

But I must say now I think he's really rising to the occasion. The way he's sticking it out and courting you –

ALAN. Ah he's a lovely fella. He really is. Even if there is almost nothing on Google about him.

CASEY. Do you really think so?

PAULINE. Absolutely.

CASEY is thrilled.

CASEY. Thank you. I appreciate you – seeing that.

PAULINE raises a glass.

PAULINE. To hell with all the statistics – I hope it all works out.

ALAN raises a glass too.

ALAN. Me too, love.

CASEY. Thanks.

PAULINE. I really really really hope it all works out.

They clink glasses.

CASEY smiles.

Three

BRETT *is banging furiously on* CYNTHIA*'s door. He seems anxious.*

BRETT. Cynthia! Cynthia! Open up! Cynthia!

ERIC comes to the door in his gym gear.

ERIC....Brett?

BRETT takes a step.

BRETT. Oh. Hey, Eric. (*Changing accent.*) Hey Eric. Is – Cynthia here?

ERIC. No.

BRETT. Do you know where she might be?

ERIC. Work maybe? Why are you –

BRETT. There was just um… there was a misunderstanding
a couple of days ago.

ERIC. With Casey?

BRETT. Well –

ERIC. Were they fighting again? So weird the way they're
fighting so much these days. Especially now Casey's so happy.

BRETT *looks up*.

BRETT. You – think Casey's happy?

ERIC. Oh yeah. Ever since she met you… Mr Perfect.

BRETT*'s pleased*.

Almost like Cynthia's jealous or something.

ERIC *laughs too loudly*.

BRETT *laughs too loudly too*.

BRETT. No…

An awkward beat.

BRETT *turns to go*.

Well. Sorry to –

ERIC (*suddenly*). I was just working out.

BRETT. Working out?

ERIC. Bought a couple of dumb-bells for the living room.
Thought I'd – ease myself in. No point forking out for a gym
membership, when you get the same results at home.

BRETT. Oh. (*Then*.) Good for you.

ERIC *nods*.

BRETT *moves to leave*.

ERIC. You could give me a hand. If you want. Cos like, you
know what you're doing with all this fitness stuff. And I'm
just… a novice.

BRETT. I don't really know what I'm –

ERIC. Just five minutes.

BRETT *concedes reluctantly.*

BRETT.…Okay.

They go inside.

ERIC *sits down on the ground, enthusiastic.*

ERIC. I was just doing some sit-ups.

He puts his hand behind his ears and does a sit-up.

Like this… Easy-peasy.

BRETT *looks at his watch and then around, distracted.*

BRETT.…Yeah.

ERIC. I was really unfit at first but now I'm really…

He struggles.

…nailing it. You know?

BRETT *watches him. Then –*

BRETT. If you put your hands like this it makes it harder.

ERIC. What?

BRETT. Like this.

BRETT *lies down and demonstrates.*

ERIC *watches, a little amazed.*

ERIC. Oh… cool.

BRETT. Now you try.

ERIC *does the sit-up with the new hand position.*

Harder right?

ERIC.…Yeah. Yeah. That's… hard.

Every time ERIC *comes up, he might come a little closer to* BRETT*'s face.*

BRETT. If I hold your legs, it'll steady you.

BRETT *places his hands on* ERIC*'s legs.*

ERIC. Will it yeah?

BRETT....See?

    ERIC *sits up, still coming closer to* BRETT.

ERIC....Yeah.

BRETT. Good?

ERIC....Yeah. (*Then*.) That's... that's great.

    ERIC *continues to do the sit-ups, still coming close to* BRETT *each time.*

    It's funny cos when I first met Cynthia, she was so – understanding, you know? Like she'd go to the doctor with Casey, she'd make sure she got out of the house. It was beautiful, really. How devoted she was. Kind of what made me fall in love with her. Her compassion.

    ERIC *stops, looks at* BRETT*, then suddenly leans forward like he's about to kiss him.*

    BRETT *moves subtly away.*

BRETT. Okay.

    ERIC *quickly continues doing sit-ups.*

ERIC. Where did you learn all this anyway? Did you... work in a... gym or something?

BRETT....I just find exercise helps.

ERIC. Helps what?

BRETT. My – issues.

ERIC. You have issues?

BRETT. When I was younger.

ERIC. Thought you were Mr Perfect. Cynthia says –

    BRETT *shifts, uncomfortable.*

BRETT. You shouldn't listen to Cynthia. (*Then*.) You don't know when she might be –

ERIC. I think she might hate me.

BRETT. What?

    ERIC *stops doing sit-ups.*

ERIC. I can see it in her eyes. The way she looks at me with total – disgust.

BRETT. I'm sure that's not –

BRETT *shifts, deeply uncomfortable.*

ERIC. Don't blame her really. Hate myself most days. I've been tinkering around with this new pitch but I don't think it's much good.

He looks at BRETT, *genuine.*

I think I might be washed up, Brett.

A beat.

BRETT *tries to think of something to say.*

BRETT. I think… people in the West put too much emphasis on success.

ERIC. People in the West?

BRETT. Like what is success? Who measures it?

ERIC. That's a – fair point.

BRETT. We're more than what we do for a living, you know.

ERIC *looks at him, impressed.*

ERIC. Yeah… (*Then.*) What were your issues?

BRETT. Doesn't matter.

ERIC. I'd like to hear.

BRETT. It's in the past.

ERIC. Might help me feel better though…

He looks at BRETT *like a helpless puppy. And* BRETT *feels like he has no choice.*

BRETT. It was just some… anger stuff. When I was young.

ERIC. Anger stuff?

BRETT. Aggression.

ERIC (*gripped*). *Aggression?*

BRETT. I punched a guy.

ERIC. Fuck off.

BRETT. A few guys. Broke one's arm, another's leg…
   another's jaw.

ERIC. Jesus.

   ERIC *reflexively puts his hand to his jaw.*

BRETT. I'm not proud of it.

ERIC. No.

BRETT. It's terrible… it's a terrible way to –

ERIC. Yeah.

BRETT. But it felt good.

ERIC. Did it yeah?

BRETT. At the time… I was a little – different to the other kids.
   My dad didn't really get me. He used to beat me up.

ERIC. God.

BRETT. I got expelled.

ERIC. Why?

   BRETT *glances at him.*

BRETT. There was an – incident at school – well a couple of
   incidents… guess they felt they had to. Anyway, things got
   bad after that. Dad got more violent, I got more violent. Just
   felt like the easiest way to –

ERIC. Let off steam.

BRETT. Right.

   ERIC *looks at him, admiring.*

ERIC. Maybe I should try?

BRETT. No!

ERIC. I was just – [joking.]

BRETT. I spent some time in a…

   ERIC *thinks, then realises.*

ERIC. Oh… *prison*?

  Does Casey know?

BRETT (*quickly*). No one knows!

ERIC. Okay.

BRETT (*slightly aggressive*). And I don't want anyone *to* know.

ERIC (*nervous*). I won't breathe a… word. /

BRETT. It's in the past. I've turned my life around. I met someone who helped me turn my life around. He gave me a job, he talked about Eastern philosophy.

ERIC. Eastern philosophy?

BRETT. I'm not that guy any more. And neither are you.

  ERIC *looks at him.*

ERIC.…What?

BRETT. The failed producer with the dissatisfied wife. You're not that guy.

ERIC. Oh.

  ERIC *looks down, visibly hurt.*

  Oh right. Okay.

BRETT. I just meant…

  BRETT *wants to help.*

  …I heard this thing once – that long-time spouses find their partners more attractive in unfamiliar situations. Like – when they're giving a talk or – holding court in roomful of strangers. Or when they do something really surprising. Something they'd never normally do at home.

ERIC. You think I should do something surprising?

BRETT. Well that's – up to you. The point is you don't have to accept anyone else's idea of you, Eric.

  ERIC *nods, mulling.*

ERIC. No…

BRETT. You can change.

ERIC *nods. He feels kind of moved by this.*

ERIC. Right. Yeah… thanks, bro.

BRETT *nods.*

BRETT. No problem.

ERIC *hugs him… Then maybe leans in for another kiss.*

BRETT *side-steps – it's unclear as to whether he's registered it or not.*

Better go. Casey's waiting.

ERIC. Yeah, course…

Then –

…why were you looking for Cynthia again?

BRETT *stops. A brief beat.*

BRETT. Don't worry about it.

BRETT *goes.*

ERIC *looks at his hands.*

Then he makes a fist and punches the air.

Four

CASEY *is in her flat.*

She wears a silk nightdress and is lighting some candles. Maybe some music plays.

BRETT *enters. He turns on the lights.*

CASEY. Hey.

BRETT. What happened to all the…

CASEY. Quick turn them off.

BRETT *turns off the lights.*

It's supposed to be romantic.

BRETT looks around.

BRETT.... Where's all the furniture, Casey?

CASEY. I had some bills to pay.

BRETT.... You sold it?

CASEY. We can buy it back. In a few months.

He stares at her in shock.

BRETT. I didn't know you were having –

CASEY. Don't worry about it. We're both making sacrifices.

CASEY comes towards him, seductive.

I have a shift in a few hours so... we should make the most of our time.

She kisses him.

Did you get my email?

BRETT. No.

CASEY. I wrote a new... [story.]

BRETT. Oh.

She hands him some paper. A script.

CASEY. I was worried you were getting bored. With the same old same old. And me being so clingy and annoying –

BRETT. You weren't – clingy and –

CASEY. Yes I was. I was being crazy. And I'm sorry. It's because of Cynthia – I was letting her get to me. Which is stupid. Cos this is nothing to do with her. *This* is the one thing she can't affect so...

BRETT looks down, ashamed.

She puts her hand on him.

I just want to reassure you, it's not going to be like that when we're married.

BRETT. I have to tell you something.

CASEY (*excited*). Have a read first – I think you'll like it.

BRETT. Something happened.

CASEY. What?

She looks at the pages.

Wait. Are you still working off the old one cos this is – better.

BRETT. With Cynthia.

CASEY.…Cynthia?

She stops. Looks at him.

BRETT. I didn't mean it, I swear to god.

And suddenly she realises.

CASEY.…Oh.

She takes a shocked step, back.

BRETT. I just got carried away in the moment. I lost control.

She looks at him.

But it was nothing – all we did was –

CASEY *puts her hand up.*

CASEY. Stop.

She tries to gather herself.

BRETT. Casey…

She doesn't move.

Casey, please –

CASEY (*quietly*). I'd like you to read the new story.

BRETT.…but I want to tell you –

CASEY. I don't want you to tell me.

BRETT. But – I think we should talk about it.

CASEY. I don't want to talk about it. I want to read the new story.

BRETT. Casey –

CASEY. That's an old story, Brett. I've been living *that* story all my life. I want *this* story. So can you please just do your job and read what's on the page.

Her voice cracks. BRETT *looks at her, hurt.*

BRETT. Casey –

CASEY. Just do what I pay you for, Brett!

BRETT stops, shocked. He looks down at the page.

He takes a breath and tries to read his lines.

BRETT. You look – you look beautiful in that nightdress.

CASEY nods, fighting back tears.

CASEY. Thank you. I bought it for you. You're late.

BRETT watches her, upset, but keeps reading.

BRETT. I know. I've been – digging all night. My hands are sore and calloused. I thought I was tired but looking at you…

CASEY (*choking back tears*). You should have an early night.

BRETT (*reading*). Screw the early night!

He stops.

Sorry – was that too…

CASEY shakes her head, still trying not to cry.

CASEY. Keep going.

BRETT (*reading*). I want you. I've never wanted anything more in my life I won't take no for an answer – (*To* CASEY.) Is that a bit…

CASEY. Just keep going.

BRETT reads the stage directions.

BRETT. …It says to lift you up.

She nods.

He comes towards her, trying.

(*Reading.*) I'm taking you upstairs right now.

CASEY lets out a little sob. BRETT *stops.*

(*To* CASEY, *worried.*) Are you sure you're okay with this?

CASEY *nods, upset.*

Cos I just feel like we should –

CASEY. Just keep going, Brett.

BRETT. But you're crying.

CASEY. Please, Brett. Can we just stick to the new story? I want to stick to the new story.

He looks at her, helpless.

Tears are streaming down CASEY'*s face.*

BRETT....I'm a good guy, Casey. I don't want to hurt you.

CASEY....Then why did you kiss my sister?

BRETT *takes that in.*

They look at one another in the candlelight.

Then BRETT *picks her up, and carries her out of the room in his arms.*

Five

CYNTHIA *and* ERIC'*s bedroom.*

CYNTHIA *is pacing in her nightdress, turning* SEBASTIAN'*s card over in her hands.*

ERIC *comes to the door wearing a jacket, tight pants and sunglasses.*

He leans against something, trying to be sexy.

ERIC. Knock knock...

CYNTHIA *turns, slightly wild-eyed.*

CYNTHIA. I just remembered the Kinsellas.

ERIC'*s caught slightly off-guard.*

ERIC....The – Sharon and David?

CYNTHIA. He said she dropped her bag on his foot in Venice airport waiting for the waterbus and that's how they first met.

ERIC. Yeah…

CYNTHIA. Yeah right! Far too perfect. Who meets like that?

ERIC. I thought you were getting ready for – bed.

CYNTHIA. I am ready.

ERIC. But I thought we were gonna…

He gestures to the bed.

CYNTHIA. Oh. Right.

ERIC. I mean we don't have to –

CYNTHIA. No, no we can – give it a… go.

She goes to the bed and lies down perfunctorily.

ERIC comes towards her trying to be sultry. Maybe he crawls onto the bed.

ERIC. …Do you like my pants?

CYNTHIA glances at his pants.

CYNTHIA. They're a bit tight.

ERIC. …Sexy kind of tight?

CYNTHIA (*suddenly*). Susan and what's his name – Jake!

ERIC stops.

ERIC. Jake?

CYNTHIA sits up, excited.

CYNTHIA. She said they met in a lift that got stuck.

ERIC. Yeah, she was having a panic attack and he talked her down.

CYNTHIA. Bullshit!

ERIC. They told the story at the wedding.

CYNTHIA. But it's bullshit. I've seen that scene in a film!

ERIC's not sure what's going on.

(*To herself.*) Maybe everyone is doing this? Maybe all of it's a fake? I mean every story you hear at a wedding has the same formula. They meet, there's some obstacle – like he thinks she doesn't like him or she's leaving the country the next day blah blah – they get married.

ERIC *tries to get things back on track. He leans into her.*

ERIC. We didn't have an obstacle. For us it was love at first sight.

CYNTHIA. How could it have been love at first sight? You didn't know the first thing about me – I could have been a murderer.

ERIC.…I got the sense.

CYNTHIA. You projected! It didn't matter who I was. You were living out a story, I just fit a part in your head.

ERIC *is desperately trying to keep things on track.*

ERIC. I was actually thinking we could try some role play… These are the trousers I wore the day we first met – when I was a big hotshot producer…

CYNTHIA. So you're role-playing – yourself?

ERIC *realises this is a stupid idea. He takes off the sunglasses.*

ERIC. Or I can be someone else. What about a masseur? Or a plumber or – a tall dark handsome –

CYNTHIA *throws herself back on the bed in despair.*

CYNTHIA. God it's all so derivative.

ERIC.…What?

CYNTHIA. Everything. Love. Sex – it's just one big cliché. The only way we could possibly know something is real is…

She stops, some realisation dawning.

Oh my god.

ERIC. Listen, Cynthia – I think we really need to make more of a –

CYNTHIA *pushes him off and her and jumps out of bed.*

CYNTHIA. I have to go out.

ERIC. It's eleven o'clock.

She puts on some shoes, flustered.

CYNTHIA. I need some air.

ERIC. But we were just about to –

CYNTHIA. I won't be long...

ERIC. Cynthia! I was really hoping we could – Cynthia!

But she's gone.

He throws his sunglasses down and sits on the bed, defeated.

A beat.

...God these pants are tight.

Six

A phone ringing.

ALAN *and* PAULINE *in their different houses.*

PAULINE *is ringing.* ALAN *answers.*

ALAN. Hello?

PAULINE *doesn't speak.*

...Who is this?

Beat.

It's almost midnight... Look, you can't keep doing this. This is harassment. You're upsetting my wife... Hello?

He slams the phone down and walks off.

PAULINE *stands, cradling the receiver in her hands.*

A beat then –

PAULINE....Hello?

Seven

A park at night.

CYNTHIA *is pacing, jittery, manic.*

BRETT *arrives, tense, hands in pockets.*

CYNTHIA. Oh thank god I didn't think you were coming.

BRETT. You can't call this late at night.

CYNTHIA. You smell nice.

> *She moves to kiss him. He moves away.*

BRETT. It's not fair on Casey.

CYNTHIA. I haven't stopped thinking about you. Haven't been able to eat. Haven't been able to sleep. Everyone at work thinks it's some kind of detox.

BRETT (*awkward*). Look, I just came to apologise for the other day. It was… inexcusable.

CYNTHIA. Don't talk in that voice.

BRETT. This is my voice.

CYNTHIA. Be yourself when you're with me. (*Then*.) You have to leave Casey.

BRETT.… What?

CYNTHIA. I'll leave Eric.

BRETT. What are you – talking about?

CYNTHIA. We're in love.

> BRETT*'s shocked.*

BRETT. We had – one kiss.

CYNTHIA. Well it was real. It's the only thing that is.

BRETT. I just came to say sorry.

CYNTHIA. I've been thinking about it – you're an actor.

> BRETT *recoils, shocked.*

BRETT. What?

CYNTHIA. You're being paid to play a part.

BRETT. How do you – know about –

CYNTHIA. Yes or no?

BRETT. Where did you –

CYNTHIA. Just answer the question, Brett, yes or no?

BRETT. Well, okay but –

CYNTHIA. Okay! So that kiss wasn't part of the story.

BRETT. Cynthia, please –

CYNTHIA. That came from you. Which makes it true.

BRETT. It was a mistake.

CYNTHIA. You want me.

BRETT. No.

CYNTHIA. You went off-script.

    BRETT*'s visibly stressed.*

BRETT. I got – carried away.

    CYNTHIA *moves close to him.*

CYNTHIA. You said we had a connection.

BRETT. Yeah but –

CYNTHIA. You said it felt deep.

BRETT. It – did – in the moment.

CYNTHIA. So if you felt it –

BRETT. As him.

CYNTHIA. But *you* still felt it.

BRETT. I was playing a part.

CYNTHIA. But it's you in that part, you're still you.

BRETT. There's a difference.

CYNTHIA. What difference?

    And BRETT *is suddenly at a loss.*

BRETT. Oh god, I'm so confused. This wasn't supposed to happen.

BRETT *puts his head in his hands, upset.*

CYNTHIA *takes his hand, starts to stroke his arm.*

CYNTHIA. Shhhhhh it's okay /

BRETT. I'm a fucking failure.

Suddenly he kicks something, angry.

CYNTHIA. I went to see your boss.

He stops.

I called the number on that card.

BRETT. You – what?

CYNTHIA. There's a way out of your contract. Well, actually there are several ways out of the contract.

BRETT. You went to see Sebastian?

CYNTHIA. The first is if you hurt yourself, but that would be awful. The second is if Casey terminates the contract, which has to be done twenty-four hours before the wedding or she incurs a major cost. You should see their price lists – mad! She's basically taken a mortgage.

BRETT. What have you done?

CYNTHIA. They can't expect you to *actually* marry her.

BRETT. This is my life, Cynthia.

CYNTHIA. And it's *for* life. Are you really ready to do that to yourself?

BRETT. …Yes. Yes I… I *want* to be – ready. I want to be able to –

CYNTHIA. You're a human being, Brett, not some two-dimensional pin-up. When you were talking about nooses and being hemmed in, you were talking about you.

BRETT. No I –

CYNTHIA. *You're* the one who's trapped.

BRETT *is panicked and confused.*

BRETT. …Am I?

CYNTHIA. You will be if you marry her… You have to end it.

BRETT. But… it'll break her heart.

CYNTHIA. She's living a lie… We have something real, Brett – I know we do cos –

She stops, suddenly and looks at him.

For god's sake will you just tell me your actual name.

Eight

CASEY *in a wedding shop, wearing a wedding dress.*

She looks unhappy.

PAULINE *appears and clasps her hands together, moved at the sight of her.*

PAULINE. Oh, Casey! I never thought I'd see the day.

CASEY. It's not sitting right.

CASEY *pulls at the dress, agitated.*

PAULINE. You look beautiful!

CASEY. I look fat.

PAULINE *looks at her, shocked.*

PAULINE. … Are you having one of your bad days?

CASEY. I'm thinking of not inviting Cynthia to the wedding.

PAULINE. Casey! She's your sister. I don't even know what you're fighting about.

CASEY *pulls at the dress again.*

CASEY. I don't like this any more. It's too fussy.

PAULINE. What's gotten into you?

CASEY (*suddenly*). Did Dad tell you he was cheating?

PAULINE. Pardon?

CASEY. Or did he just sneak around behind your back?

PAULINE. Why are you asking this now?

CASEY. I'm just wondering. How did you find out he was being unfaithful, did he tell you or did you suspect?

PAULINE. Well, bit of both I suppose.

PAULINE *shrugs*.

I mean he has his dalliances, your father, but he always comes back.

CASEY *glances at her*.

CASEY.... You mean he always – came back.

PAULINE. Look at Barbara, for god's sake.

CASEY. Barbara's his wife.

PAULINE *gives a little laugh*.

PAULINE. And a 'nutritionist' apparently. Don't know how he keeps a straight face.

CASEY *frowns*.

CASEY. She *is* a nutritionist. She's very highly qualified.

PAULINE. It won't last.

CASEY. It *has* lasted. Three years.

PAULINE. Well we had thirty, so.

CASEY. And he was cheating. And you were miserable.

PAULINE. Not for all of it. You don't spend thirty years with someone and not know their routines, Casey. If he thinks some – vitamin supplier is going to bring him happiness in his twilight years – fine. Let him think it. I know better.

CASEY *stares at her, disbelief*.

CASEY. He left you.

PAULINE. Yes.

CASEY. So he didn't want to be with you any more.

PAULINE. He *thinks* he doesn't want to be with me any more.

CASEY. He's married someone else.

PAULINE. I don't like that tone.

CASEY. You're sounding insane!

PAULINE. Well that's rich coming from you.

CASEY steps back, hurt.

CASEY (*hurt*)….What did you say?

PAULINE gets up, unsettled. Starts fussing with something.

PAULINE. You've an illness, Casey. You don't see things straight. I don't expect you to understand.

CASEY stares at PAULINE, wounded.

CASEY. But I *do* understand. I do understand – love.

PAULINE. You know deep down if someone is meant for you. Even if they don't know it themselves. *You* know and that's what matters. You don't just throw it all away because of a few – nutritionists. You hang in there. You persevere.

(*Passionate.*) 'Love is not love
Which alters when it alteration finds,
Or bends with the remover to remove.
Oh no! it is an ever fixed mark,
That looks on tempests and is *never* shaken.'

That's love, Casey. That's Shakespeare.

A silence.

CASEY stares at PAULINE, something finally dawning on her.

PAULINE looks at CASEY's dress.

I agree with you about the dress. Bit tight around the hips. Let's talk to the girl, see if they can let it out by Saturday.

PAULINE moves off into the shop.

CASEY is left alone.

She walks to the mirror and looks at herself.

A long beat.

Then very slowly she reaches up and pulls off the veil.

Nine

Wedding music. PAULINE*'s place.*

A table set for dinner. Confetti, heart-shaped balloons, the works.

PAULINE *is standing on a chair, hanging bunting, while*
ALAN *is fiddling with a stereo playing 'Here Comes the Bride'.*

ALAN. Dearly beloved, we are gathered here today in the sight of god /

PAULINE. Turn that down. /

ALAN. To join this man and this – woman.

PAULINE. It's too loud, Alan.

ALAN. In holy matrimony.

PAULINE. It's not holy.

ALAN. What?

He turns it down.

PAULINE. They're not doing a holy one. It's a civil what's-it-called.

ALAN. Well it's definitely more civilised than the last one we had. Renting that castle –

PAULINE. Bunratty.

ALAN. Bunrobbery.

They laugh.

ERIC *enters. He's wearing a leather jacket, carrying a bottle of wine. He looks well.*

ERIC. Is this where it's all happening?

PAULINE. Eric! Look at you.

PAULINE *comes down to assess him.*

ERIC (*bashful*). What?

PAULINE. The hair and the jacket. It's very –

ALAN. Brett.

PAULINE. Yes, actually.

ERIC *doesn't mind this comparison.*

ERIC. Well I wasn't really sure what to wear to be honest. Never really got the point of a rehearsal dinner.

ALAN. Me neither.

ERIC. I mean what are we rehearsing?

ALAN. You can't rehearse life.

They laugh.

PAULINE. It's just to make sure everything goes smoothly and to meet the registrar – she's young apparently.

ERIC. And are Brett's family here?

ALAN *shakes his head.*

PAULINE. Too far to travel.

ERIC. S'pose, they're not that close anyway.

PAULINE. Are they not? How do you know?

ERIC. Brett mentioned it.

ALAN (*intrigued*). Did he? When?

ERIC. Oh just in private. Man to man.

ALAN. You know more than us so. Like blood from a stone getting anything out of him.

ERIC *smiles, pleased with his knowledge.*

ERIC. Well I don't know much. He had a few issues with his dad.

PAULINE. Issues? /

ALAN. His dad?

PAULINE *and* ALAN *move in for a gossip as* BRETT *enters. He seems tense –*

BRETT. Have you guys seen Casey?

They spring apart.

ERIC. There he is! Man of the match.

PAULINE. You're looking very smart, Brett.

BRETT. Thank you.

He looks around the room at all the decorations, seems slightly overwhelmed.

PAULINE. She must be upstairs.

BRETT. I'll check.

BRETT *starts to head out.* ALAN *holds out a beer –*

ALAN. Here. Have a drink.

BRETT. No thanks, Mr Cassidy.

ERIC. Nerves at you?

ERIC *playfully punches him.*

Pressure's on now, eh?

BRETT. Eh yeah.

BRETT *rushes out.*

PAULINE. He looks a bit pale.

ALAN. He looks fine.

ERIC. Always think he looks a bit orange – is that fake tan?

PAULINE. I often think Barbara looks a bit orange. But then she drinks a lot of carrot juice. Is she coming today, Alan?

ALAN. Barbara? No. She's – having some trouble with her back.

ERIC. Her back?

PAULINE. It's those small bones. They crumble like chalk.

ALAN. She'll be here tomorrow.

PAULINE. She won't age well.

ALAN (*annoyed*). Eric, how's work?

ERIC. Oh grand, yeah.

ALAN. You're still doing the thing with the – orphans?

ERIC. Eh no, actually, no. I've – left that to one side.

ALAN. You've abandoned the orphans?

ERIC. I think people in the West are too – focused on success.

PAULINE. People in the West?

ERIC. We're more than what we do for a living. You know?

ERIC doesn't seem entirely convinced by this.

ALAN. True… (*Then.*) But some people have a vocation, don't they? Like what they do is… why they're here?

ERIC hadn't thought about this. He awkwardly holds up some wine.

ERIC. Have you an opener for this?

PAULINE. In the kitchen.

ERIC. Thanks – (*Re: the wine.*) It's Spanish.

ERIC goes. BRETT *come back in, anxious.*

BRETT. She's not up there.

ALAN. Huh?

BRETT. Casey, she's not upstairs. I've looked all over.

ALAN. Well she can't have gone far.

PAULINE. The registrar's due any minute.

BRETT. I really need to speak to her.

PAULINE. She'll be back.

BRETT. It's very very important.

ALAN laughs.

ALAN. Not having second thoughts, are you?

BRETT doesn't laugh. He looks worried.

BRETT. …I'll look outside again.

BRETT hurries out.

ALAN shakes his head.

ALAN. …I dunno.

He takes a seat at the far side of the room.

He looks around and realises PAULINE *is studying him intently.*

…What?

She comes over and perches beside him. He shifts, uncomfortable.

PAULINE. Are things a bit difficult at the moment, Alan?

ALAN. Difficult?

PAULINE. With Barbara.

ALAN....No.

PAULINE. She never comes with you to any of these things.

ALAN. It's a rehearsal dinner.

PAULINE. You can't rehearse life.

ALAN. *I* said that. Everything's grand between me and Barbara.

PAULINE *places a hand on his arm, looks at him, intense.*

PAULINE. I'm always here for you. You know that, don't you?

He looks at her hand.

You can tell me anything. If you're having problems with your new wife, I'd absolutely love to hear about them.

CYNTHIA *rushes in carrying flowers, a wild look in her eyes.*

CYNTHIA. Sorry we're late.

ALAN *jumps up, relieved.*

ALAN. You're just in time.

CYNTHIA. Where is everyone?

PAULINE. Well, Casey's missing and Brett's popped out.

CYNTHIA. What?

PAULINE. But they'll be back. Who's this?

A small man in a crumpled linen jacket steps awkwardly out from behind CYNTHIA.

DAVE. Hi, I'm Dave...

He puts out his hand.

PAULINE. Dave?

CYNTHIA. He's joining us for dinner.

PAULINE. Does Casey know?

DAVE (*uncertain*). Are you sure this is alright?

CYNTHIA. Course it's alright. Sit down, Dave. Relax. Dad, give him a drink.

> DAVE *awkwardly takes a seat as* ALAN *hands him a beer.*

PAULINE. Cynthia, Casey's very fragile at the moment.

CYNTHIA. It's fine, Mom. Don't worry about it.

> ERIC *enters.*

ERIC. Cynthia!

CYNTHIA. Eric! You're – here?

ERIC. Why wouldn't I be here?

CYNTHIA. Did you not get my note?

ERIC. Yeah but I had to meditate before I left so I didn't read it. Drink?

> *He holds up the wine and some glasses.* CYNTHIA *stares at him, stunned.*

CYNTHIA.… Yes, please.

> ERIC *pours her a drink.* CYNTHIA *knocks it back.*

> DAVE *introduces himself to* ERIC.

DAVE. Hi, I'm Dave.

CYNTHIA. Eric's a producer.

DAVE (*interested*). Oh. Factual or – drama?

ERIC (*confused*). Are you a friend of Brett's?

DAVE. Who's Brett?

CYNTHIA. Dave's a crime writer. He writes very successful books under a pseudonym.

ALAN. What pseudonym?

DAVE. David Darkness.

PAULINE. I've heard of him.

DAVE. They're quite popular in the Midlands. (*To* ERIC, *pointed*.) Here's my card. I think they'd work really well for television.

ERIC. Right.

PAULINE. Cynthia, could I have a little word?

CYNTHIA *cuts across her.*

CYNTHIA. Not now. So it's hard to meet people, would you say, Dave? In your line of work?

DAVE *looks a little disgruntled.*

DAVE. It can be – difficult, yes. A writer's life is a sedentary life. But luckily I've a wonderful partner.

CYNTHIA (*eager*). Yes, yes tell us about your partner, Dave.

DAVE. Well I'd prefer to discuss my work…

ERIC. Work's overrated.

CYNTHIA. And we'd love to hear, I'm sure you've a fabulous story about how you met.

DAVE *looks around, a little uncertain now.*

DAVE. Well –

CYNTHIA. Start from the beginning.

PAULINE. Cynthia.

CYNTHIA *waves for her to shut up.*

DAVE. His name's… Raphael. He's Italian.

CYNTHIA. Italian!

DAVE. A pilot.

CYNTHIA. Pilot! So he's away a lot?

DAVE. I only see him once a fortnight, but I don't mind.

ERIC. If it works for you, it works for you.

CYNTHIA. And what does he look like this – *Raphael*?

DAVE. Oh very striking. Dark burnished hair. About six-two. Sort of – butch.

CYNTHIA*'s behaviour seems increasingly manic.*

CYNTHIA. He sounds great. Sounds quite familiar actually. He sounds like someone *closer to home*.

ERIC. Well I wouldn't call myself butch.

CYNTHIA. Brett. He sounds like Brett.

ERIC. Oh.

ERIC *pulls a note out of his pocket.*

Oh look! Just found your note.

CYNTHIA (*alarmed*). What?

ERIC. Must have just put it in my pocket. (*To* DAVE.) Cynthia and I used to write each other notes all the time when we first met.

PAULINE. Isn't that lovely?

ERIC. It *was* kind of romantic.

CYNTHIA (*nervous*). Well don't read it now.

ERIC *smiles.*

ERIC. Why? Is it embarrassing?

CYNTHIA. It's just – silly.

She tries to grab it. He holds it away thinking it's a game.

ERIC. Like saucy – silly.

CYNTHIA. Don't be stupid.

ERIC. So I can read it out.

CYNTHIA (*desperate*). No!

ERIC. Pauline and Alan won't be shocked.

CYNTHIA. Please.

ERIC. I'll stop if it gets too…

ALAN. Please.

He starts to read.

ERIC. Dear Eric.

PAULINE. Good start.

ERIC. …I've met someone else.

A stunned silence.

…Sorry if this hurts you, but our marriage is over. I wish you well.

A very long beat. ERIC *stares at the page.*

…I wish you well?

CYNTHIA. I'm not good at endings.

ALAN (*whispering to* PAULINE). Is this a joke?

CYNTHIA. No, Dad, it's not a joke.

ERIC. Oh my god.

CYNTHIA. Okay can we just –

ERIC. I mean I knew we were having problems but…

CYNTHIA. This is Casey's wedding rehearsal, let's think about her.

He looks at the note.

ERIC. That's it? That's the last five years? 'I wish you well.'

CYNTHIA. Well what do you want me to say?

ERIC. Anything. I'd like you to have said anything. I'd like you to have told me.

CYNTHIA. I *was* telling you, Eric. Every day of our miserable marriage.

DAVE *leans over and awkwardly whispers to* CYNTHIA.

DAVE. Excuse me, you said this was a networking lunch for media types.

CYNTHIA. Eric is a media type!

ERIC. Who is it? The guy you're fucking?

CYNTHIA. I'm not – fucking anyone.

ERIC. Is it him?

He points to DAVE.

DAVE. Me!

ALAN. No he's got Raphael.

DAVE. Exactly!

CYNTHIA. Which is why I brought him. I wanted him to meet Brett.

DAVE. Who's Brett?

ERIC (*frustrated*). Who's the guy who's ended our marriage, Cynthia?

BRETT *enters –*

BRETT. Okay I don't know what's happened but Casey is nowhere to be –

CYNTHIA. Brett!

DAVE. Raphael!

BRETT. Dave? Ciao. I mean – (*Shocked.*) what?

ALAN *leans into* PAULINE.

ALAN. Is he talking in an accent?

PAULINE (*whispering*). Does he think Brett is Raphael?

CYNTHIA (*excited*). Brett *is* Raphael. That's why I brought Dave here.

DAVE. What? You lied.

CYNTHIA. I just wanted everyone to understand –

TESS *enters, looking officious.*

TESS. Hi I'm Tess, I'm the registrar.

SEBASTIAN*'s behind her.*

SEBASTIAN. And I'm Sebastian, the – celebrant.

PAULINE *rushes over.*

PAULINE. Oh hello.

BRETT (*panicked*). Oh god…

PAULINE. You've come at a bit of a funny – time.

CYNTHIA (*pointing*). She's not a registrar!

TESS *looks startled*.

TESS. Yes I am. I have the paperwork.

CYNTHIA. They run a company. They hire actors to pretend to be people's boyfriends or girlfriends or whatever. They charge a fortune.

BRETT. Cynthia –

SEBASTIAN (*to* CYNTHIA). You need to be careful.

CYNTHIA. Brett is an actor.

PAULINE. Is he not a gardener?

DAVE. No he's a pilot. Isn't that right, Raphael?

TESS (*to* CYNTHIA). Can I remind *some* people here that they've signed legal documents?

ALAN. I have no idea what is going on right now.

CYNTHIA. This wedding is a sham. Casey cannot marry Brett, because she hired him. And so did Dave.

PAULINE. So he *is* a prostitute?

SEBASTIAN. Is an artist a prostitute if he sells his work?

TESS. Sebastian.

DAVE (*to* TESS). This is absolutely appalling. I'm a successful crime writer with a reputation to maintain. I was promised discretion.

TESS (*to* CYNTHIA). *You* are in breach of contract.

CYNTHIA. And your company turns people into human timeshares.

Suddenly ERIC *picks up a chair and hurls it across the room*.

ERIC. WILL YOU JUST TELL ME WHO HE FUCKING IS???

Everyone stops.

Who is the man you're leaving me for, Cynthia?

A long beat. Everyone looks at CYNTHIA.

CYNTHIA.…it's Brett.

Everyone – including BRETT *– gasps*.

ERIC. Brett?

CYNTHIA. We kissed. A few days ago. And he wasn't acting. It was real. It happened spontaneously. And it woke something inside me, something, Eric, that I haven't felt for a very long time.

BRETT. Cynthia, I really don't think you should've…

And suddenly ERIC *lunges for* BRETT.

ERIC. I'm gonna fucking kill you!

PAULINE *and* ALAN *hold him back*.

PAULINE. Oh my god.

ERIC. I'm gonna break your stupid pretty-boy face.

CYNTHIA. Oh now you grow a pair of balls.

ERIC. Come on!

DAVE. I'm sorry I'm very uneasy with physical violence.

TESS. You write crime novels.

ERIC. Just let me at him. Let me fucking at him.

ERIC *suddenly breaks through*.

DAVE. Raphael!

PAULINE *and* ALAN *stop* ERIC *again*.

ALAN. Eric, come on.

DAVE. That's it, I'm terminating this contract.

DAVE *rushes for the door.*

TESS *rushes after him desperately.*

TESS. No wait. We'll find you someone else.

DAVE. I did not sign up for public humiliation.

TESS. Someone better –

DAVE. I just wanted a TV dramatisation of one of my books.

TESS. But –

DAVE. It's not like people are sick to death of crime drama!

He runs out. Before TESS *follows, she turns to* SEBASTIAN.

TESS. Sebastian, deal with this. But don't do anything –
creative.

As TESS *goes,* ERIC *suddenly lunges for* BRETT. *They fall
to the floor.*

ERIC. AAAGGGGGGH.

CYNTHIA. For god's sake, Eric, get up. You're not fit enough.

And suddenly ERIC*'s rage turns to devastation and he
collapses into* BRETT*'s arms sobbing like a child.*

BRETT.…Eric?

BRETT *awkwardly puts his arms around* ERIC.

ERIC. How could you do this to me. I thought we were bros.

BRETT. We *are* – bros.

ERIC. I listened to you. I was going to do what you said and
surprise her.

CYNTHIA. Surprise me?

SEBASTIAN (*intrigued*). What were you going to do?

ERIC. Take her to Australia.

SEBASTIAN (*disappointed*). Oh.

ERIC *looks at* CYNTHIA.

ERIC. I thought we could get away from everything. From
work and life and just – be together – like we used to.

CYNTHIA. You used to be somebody, Eric! You used to have
a job.

ERIC. Is that the only reason you loved me?

CYNTHIA *doesn't respond.*

ERIC *stares at her, wounded. Then dramatically points
to* BRETT.

Well he's been in jail.

Everyone gasps.

BRETT (*betrayed*). That was a secret.

ERIC. Yeah well, never bite a snake cos you'll be bitten yourself, isn't that right, Pauline?

PAULINE. Certainly is.

CYNTHIA. Look all I know is – I want out of this trap. And I want to help Brett out of his trap. And then when we're both free, maybe…

CYNTHIA *looks at* BRETT, *earnest.*

Maybe we can try and… give things a go? Together?

PAULINE. But what about Casey? He's her fiancé.

A voice from behind.

CASEY. It's okay.

Everyone turns.

BRETT. Casey… How long have you been standing there?

CASEY *comes into the room.*

CASEY. Long enough.

ALAN. So you heard about Raphael?

PAULINE. Tell me it's not true, Casey, tell me Brett isn't an actor and you didn't hire him to pretend to be your boyfriend.

CASEY *looks down. And takes a deep breath.*

CASEY.…it is true.

PAULINE. Oh dear Jesus /

CASEY. Brett is an actor. I did hire him to play my boyfriend.

PAULINE. Oh Alan. I knew she shouldn't have reduced her medication.

CASEY *looks up.*

CASEY. No, see, *no.* I am *so* sick of being spoken to like that. I am so sick of being – sick. Yes I have an illness. And yes I have good days and bad days and I'll probably have them for the rest of my life but – that's not – all I am. I wanted you to see me as someone different. Someone who could go for romantic walks in a city, or take a trip to Paris and buy scarves. I wanted you to see me as someone who a person like Brett might fall in love with.

Beat.

…And I wanted to know what that might be like for me.

She trails off.

But just because *I'd* like you to see me as that person. And just because I can sometimes, *sometimes* manage to see myself as that person… doesn't mean I ever will be.

CYNTHIA. Oh Casey. I'm so glad you're saying this. I have been really really worried about you.

CYNTHIA *goes towards* CASEY*, maybe she takes her hands.*

I didn't come here today to hurt you. I just wanted you to see sense. This thing with Brett is crazy.

CASEY.…I know.

CYNTHIA. You can't buy love, Casey. It has to come *naturally.* Be natural. That's the only way to know if it's true.

CASEY *nods.*

CASEY.…And I can't be anything other than your sad, sick sister. Cos that wouldn't work for you.

CYNTHIA (*frowns*). What?

CASEY. You've always been the successful one.

CYNTHIA. Well –

CASEY. And I've always been the –

CYNTHIA. You're not a failure, don't say that.

CASEY. Mom's the martyr, Dad's the villain. If we're not who we are, who are we, you know?

CYNTHIA. I think we're getting a bit off-topic here.

PAULINE. I'm not a martyr –

CYNTHIA. The important thing is that you see this was a huge mistake.

CASEY *looks at the room.*

CASEY. I do. And it was… and I'm sorry, everyone. I'm sorry you're here, I'm sorry I lied to you and… I'm – sorry, Brett. For what I did to you. (*To* SEBASTIAN.) I'm terminating the contract as of this minute.

SEBASTIAN *sits down and starts picking despondently at the food.*

CYNTHIA. Good girl.

CYNTHIA *hugs* CASEY.

I know this must be hard.

CASEY *breaks away from* CYNTHIA*'s embrace and starts to leave.*

BRETT. But…what about me?

Everyone turns, surprised.

CYNTHIA. Let's just give it some time, Brett, okay, there's a lot of emotion.

BRETT. But – what if I don't want to end the contract?

CYNTHIA. Sorry?

ALAN. What did he say?

BRETT. What if I – want to be with Casey?

CYNTHIA.… Well that's ridiculous.

CASEY *looks up, surprised.*

CASEY. I thought you weren't – happy with me.

CYNTHIA. *Yes* – which is why you kissed me. You said it was easy. You said it flowed.

BRETT. It did.

CYNTHIA. Cos it didn't with Casey.

BRETT. No, that's true. With Casey… it was hard.

CYNTHIA. Well then.

BRETT. But just cos something's easy, doesn't make it right.

He looks at SEBASTIAN.

SEBASTIAN. Life is suffering.

CYNTHIA. You want *to suffer*? With Casey?

SEBASTIAN. Suffering being our resistance to impermanence. But impermanence being the essence of life.

CYNTHIA. What the fuck is he talking about?

He looks at CYNTHIA.

BRETT. I kissed you because it was familiar. I knew how to be with you, it was flattering. But… I was just in my comfort zone.

CYNTHIA. Comfort zone!

BRETT. Casey challenged me. She asked questions, she wanted me to go deep. And… it scared me.

CYNTHIA (*outraged*). Casey made you pretend to be someone you're not.

BRETT. Yes.

CYNTHIA. I'd let you be the real you, from – Donaghmede or wherever.

BRETT. But I don't want to be the real me.

CYNTHIA *stares at him, shocked.*

The only thing I've ever wanted in life is to be someone else. And no one would ever let me be it. When I got out of prison –

ERIC. Told yis! /

BRETT. – I trained to be an actor. It was all I ever wanted to be, ever since I was a kid. And I was good. I got an agent, I went to auditions, only no one would give me a part.

ALAN. Cos you were in the slammer?

BRETT. No. Cos I didn't look right, or I didn't sound right or they didn't see me as right for the role. And I tried everything, cos I wanted it so bad but nothing – worked. And I felt so… Do you have any idea what it's like to have something inside of you that you desperately want to express, but no one will let you?

CASEY. Yes.

ERIC. Yes.

PAULINE. Yes.

BRETT. Casey's the one person who's let me not be myself.

ALAN (*quietly*). What about Dave?

ERIC. They only saw each other once a fortnight.

PAULINE. So hang on a minute, you were with Casey three days a week and then Dave once a fortnight –

SEBASTIAN. We've a variety of contracts.

ALAN. So is he gay, is he straight?

ERIC. I think we both know sexuality is a lot more fluid than that, Alan.

ALAN. Right, right.

　　ALAN looks down, unnerved.

　　BRETT looks at CASEY, earnest.

BRETT. I want to stay with you, Casey. If you'll let me.

　　CASEY looks at him.

CASEY. Brett that's really – sweet. But I've thought about it and… I don't want to get married any more.

　　BRETT's face falls. But CASEY seems strong, resolute.

　　One person forever… I don't think it would suit me.

　　Everyone looks at her, amazed.

　　I think I need… something else.

ALAN. What?

CASEY. I don't know.

PAULINE. But by yourself?

CASEY. I've no idea.

PAULINE. But what'll become of you, Casey?

CASEY. I haven't a clue. Guess it's a story that's not been written yet.

She laughs, a little nervous.

BRETT....But can't I still be a part of the story?

CASEY *looks at him.*

CASEY. Brett... you're a good guy –

BRETT. No I'm not. You know I'm not.

CASEY *looks at him, surprised.*

...I thought if we just got married, if I just – committed to being good forever and really really tried, all that other stuff would – disappear. But no one can be good forever. And I'm tired of being afraid of what's inside of me. (*Passionate.*) I want to let it out.

Everyone steps away a little nervously. Except CASEY, *who seems intrigued by this.*

I love your imagination, Casey. I love its scope and its scale. It excites me.

CASEY. I can't afford the contract, Brett.

BRETT. Then let's not have a contract.

CASEY*'s taken aback.*

Let's throw away the contract. What's to stop us doing what we were doing, three days a week?

CASEY. But... what will you live on?

BRETT. I'll get a job.

BRETT *looks at* SEBASTIAN.

Or – maybe I could still work at the agency the other days of the week?

SEBASTIAN *looks like he's about to say no, but then relents.*

SEBASTIAN. To be honest it's hard to find good staff.

ALAN. So you'd still be going out with other people?

PAULINE. Pretending to go out with other people.

CYNTHIA. He'd be pretending to go out with her! This is ludicrous, Brett.

But BRETT *keeps looking at* CASEY.

BRETT. It worked before.

CASEY. It – did. And I quite liked having my own space the other half the week.

BRETT. So let's try. Why not? What's to stop us?

CASEY *is visibly warming to the idea.*

CASEY....But will you still be Brett?

BRETT. I'll be whoever you want me to be.

CASEY. I like Brett.

BRETT. Me too.

CASEY. But I could change.

BRETT. I love a challenge.

BRETT *puts out his hand.*

CASEY....Will I still be Casey?

BRETT....We can make it up.

CASEY *takes his hand. She smiles.*

CYNTHIA. This is completely insane.

ERIC. *This* is a brilliant documentary.

ERIC *stands up, excited.*

This is gold. I mean *fuck* – I'm calling the station. I've got my mojo back.

ERIC *dashes out with the phone.*

CYNTHIA *looks around, incredulous.*

CYNTHIA. So what, we're all just supposed to go along with this – heteronormative lie now, are we? We're all just supposed to act like this is perfectly sane.

CASEY *and* BRETT *move closer to each other, staring into one another's eyes.*

He's not a real American. He's not a real gardener. His name isn't even Brett – we don't even know what his real name is!

CASEY. I don't care about any of that.

CYNTHIA. So there are no rules now? There are no laws – we can all just do whatever the hell we like.

CASEY. We're not hurting anyone.

BRETT. We're not breaking any laws.

CYNTHIA. What about what's real?

CASEY. This is real…

BRETT *suddenly scoops* CASEY *up into his arms, romantically.*

From somewhere music begins to play.

Balloons or glitter starts falling from the ceiling –

ALAN. What the…

PAULINE. Oh my goodness.

CASEY *looks into* BRETT*'s eyes and smiles.*

CASEY.…This is real to me.

As BRETT *carries* CASEY *across the room –*

BRETT. You're making me so happy right now… Whoever you are.

PAULINE *clasps her hands in delight.*

PAULINE. Oh Alan /

CYNTHIA *climbs on the table and starts ripping down the decorations.*

CYNTHIA (*desperate*). No no no no no no no no no –

CASEY. You're making me so happy too.

CYNTHIA. NO!

PAULINE (*excited*). They're going to kiss.

As BRETT *and* CASEY *begin to kiss passionately –*

CYNTHIA (*desperate*). *This is not real!*

ALAN. Looks kinda real.

CYNTHIA. But it's not, it's not, it's – not… it's… it's… it's –

CYNTHIA *falls to her knees on the table.*

…What about *me*?

ALAN *puts a hand on her shoulder. He pats her, sympathetic.*

ALAN.…I think maybe you need a bit of time on your own, love. For yourself.

CASEY *and* BRETT *continue to kiss, passionately.*

PAULINE *watches, amazed.*

PAULINE.…Did we ever kiss like that, Alan?

ALAN *turns.*

ALAN. You and me? Don't think so.

PAULINE.…I don't think so either.

PAULINE *slowly moves away from* ALAN, *her eyes locked on* CASEY *and* BRETT. *Something dawning on her.*

But it's what I want.

ALAN *looks at her surprised. But she's not looking at him any more.*

(*Dreamy.*) I want someone to kiss me. Just like that.

CYNTHIA *lets out a little sob.* CASEY *and* BRETT *keep kissing.*

SEBASTIAN *looks at* PAULINE. *A beat.*

Then he puts out his hand.

She looks at him, surprised.

Then she places her hand in his. And he kisses it.

Slow fade.

Epilogue

The principal's office. Afternoon.

MARCUS *comes in his school uniform, his arm in a sling.*

He sits at the desk. Then GARETH *comes in, closes the door.*

GARETH. Ah Marcus. You're here. Good good.

> GARETH *moves to his desk and takes a seat. He looks at* MARCUS, *shakes his head.*

> How small you look in those clothes. It's what they say about all the greats though, isn't it? Olivier, Gielgud... Gere. Tiny in the flesh. Charisma adds height. So that's good news.

> *Beat.*

> Sadly, I'm not here with good news. But you already know that.

> *He looks at* MARCUS, *intently.*

> Thanks to a number of parental complaints about your 'dressing' not to mention Jimmy's Donovan's leg being broken in two places after you kicked him, I think it's safe to say your time here is... up.

> GARETH *gestures to the sling.*

> Not quite as immune to those playground taunts as we thought.

> *He looks at* MARCUS.

> Oh don't look so glum. There'll be other schools. Other friends. It won't all be like this. Life is long and rich and... indifferent, yes, sometimes, to our sorrows and our pain. But it's what we do with it that counts... I was a man of the stage once myself. Had to learn to tap dance. Not much call for it these days with assembly and such. But I was good in my time if I say so... wasn't bad at all.

For a brief moment, he seems lost in his own reverie of times past.

Then looks at MARCUS.

I think there might be something there for you. Give it some thought.

MARCUS *nods.*

They look at one another. A silent understanding.

Well, I think we're done here. I've a date with a mountain of fourth-class copybooks.

He gazes at the pile on his desk despondently.

Choices, eh?

GARETH *puts a hand on* MARCUS*'s shoulder, walks him to the door.*

Give my best to your mother. I hope they're not too hard on you. I do like your mother… In an appropriate headmasterly sort of way you understand.

MARCUS *looks up at him.*

Don't lose hope, Marcus. Never lose hope. There are always other parts to play.

MARCUS *nods.* GARETH *smiles.*

MARCUS *goes.*

GARETH *walks back to his desk.*

He looks around.

The room is strangely silent.

He stands for a moment taking it in.

Then he breaks into a very small, very subtle little tap dance.

He stops, self-conscious and reaches for a copybook.

He flicks through it, starts correcting.

Beat.

He does another little tap dance, bigger, the copybook in his hand.

He looks around to make sure no one's around.

He walks to a cupboard, puts on some music and starts to dance bigger, better, impressive, amazing.

He finishes. He turns off the music.

Silence.

He breathes it in.

Then he sits down at the desk as if nothing had happened and starts correcting copybooks.

The End.